Rice Solutions

Advance Praise for Rice Solutions

Sir Sherard Cowper-Coles KCMG LVO
Former British Ambassador to Israel, Saudi Arabia and Afghanistan.

This beautifully written book is a must-read for anyone wanting to do business in the Arabian Gulf. Full of insights, and anecdotes drawn from Edward Brown's deep knowledge of and affection for, the region, it entertains as well as enlightens. I warmly commend it.

Lt Gen Sir Simon Mayall KBE CB
Former Defence Senior Advisor Middle East.

I really enjoyed it and it is very usefully and accessibly written for the lay traveller to the Gulf

Mutlaq H. Al-Morished
Former CEO TASNEE (National Industrialisation Company KSA)

It's excellent, logical and practical. I find it very insightful of the local GCC culture in general and business in specific. Highly recommended for any expat coming to this part of the world for a visit but, more importantly, for business persons who will work or do business here in GCC.

Trevor Mostyn
Islam and Democracy Lecturer, Oxford University Department of Continuing Studies

Managing projects in the Arabian Gulf demands cultural understanding, sensitivity and a practical vision. As a former British Army Officer, Edward Brown offers his guidance in this readable and down to earth book. Quoting sources from the Sufi poet Rumi to TE Lawrence, he writes with the authority of a veteran. His useful lessons and tables make the guide a valuable aide memoire for executives working in the Region.

RICE SOLUTIONS

Success In Leadership And Management In The Arabian Gulf Region

Edward Brown

Publisher's Note

Every possible effort has been made to ensure that the information contained in this book is accurate at the time of going to press, and the publishers and authors cannot accept responsibility for any errors or omissions, however caused. No responsibility for loss or damage occasioned to any person acting, or refraining from action, as a result of the material in this publication can be accepted by the editor, the publisher, or the author.

First edition published in the United Kingdom in 2024 by Ideas for Leaders Publishing, a business of IEDP Ideas for Leaders Ltd.

Apart from any fair dealing for the purposes of research or private study, or criticism or review, as permitted under the Copyright, Design and Patents Act 1988, this publication may only be reproduced, stored or transmitted, in any form or by any means, with the prior permission in writing of the publishers. Enquiries concerning reproduction should be sent to the publishers at the following address:

Ideas for Leaders Publishing
42 Moray Place
Edinburgh
EH3 6BT
www.ideasforleaders.com
info@ideasforleaders.com

ISBN
978-1-915529-36-7 – Paperback
978-1-915529-37-4 – Ebook

© Edward Brown, 2024

Cover design: www.nickmortimer.co.uk
Cover Image: Dominic Brown
www.dominicbrownphotography.co.uk
Typesetting: Sopho Tarkashvili

To my wife, Ruth, whose unfailing support and encouragement have made the journey possible.

Acknowledgements

Many people have supported me in this venture and I am most grateful to everyone, but a few require special mention. In the early days in Kuwait, Yasmeen Al Musallam and Admiral (Retired) Ahmad Al Mulla provided invaluable mentoring. Dr Najat Benchiba-Savenius edited the early drafts and provided the first encouragement to publish. In Bahrain and Saudi Arabia, Wassim Iqbal, Ewan Stirling and Tim Kingsberry all provided significant input to drafts, and Edward Corry, when we were both locked down in Saudi Arabia during Covid, spent many hours discussing the topics in the book. Sir Sherard Cowper-Coles, General Sir Simon Mayall, Mutlaq Al Morished and Trevor Mostyn all provided feedback and advice on drafts at various stages, and Jaber Hameem was a great source of local Arab knowledge. Most recently, Anne Abel-Smith provided expert publishing advice and the final edit. Roddy Millar and the team at Ideas for Leaders Publishing finally saw the potential in this book. Finally, to my wife, Ruth, who has lived with this project throughout and has been a tireless critic.

Contents

Chapter 1
Rice and Not Potatoes 1

Chapter 2
Context – Some Religion and History 11

Chapter 3
Adopting the Right Mindset 27

Chapter 4
Leadership and Islam 35

Chapter 5
Gulf Arab Culture in Business 43

Chapter 6
Gulf Arab Company Structure and Management 61

Chapter 7
Gulf Arab Leadership and Management Culture 69

Chapter 8
Cultural Behaviour in the Business Environment 77

Chapter 9
Old Ideas Out 89

Chapter 10
If Things Go Wrong 97

Chapter 11
Rice Solution 105

Bibliography 111

Author Biography 114

Recommended Reading 115

CHAPTER 1

Rice and Not Potatoes

In my earlier life as a British Army officer, I was fortunate enough to command the British Military Mission in Kuwait. In that role, I commanded a group of British officers and non-commissioned officers from the British Army, Royal Navy and Royal Air Force, providing training and mentoring for the Kuwaiti Armed Forces.

On my arrival in Kuwait, I was asked to pass a copy of my CV to the Chief of the Kuwaiti Armed Forces, a senior and much revered member of the Kuwaiti ruling family who had been imprisoned and tortured by Saddam Hussein during the Iraqi invasion and occupation of Kuwait in the early 1990s. I was soon summoned for an audience with the Chief and, after exchanging the normal pleasantries, he started gently teasing me that I had expressed an interest in cooking in my CV. This caused much amusement among his retinue of senior Kuwait Army Officers because, clearly, cooking was the sole domain of female domestic staff and not British Army Officers. We continued to discuss my future role with his Armed Forces and, as he started to wind up the discussion, I thought that he was going to return to the teasing about my cooking prowess when he asked if, in British cooking, we preferred potatoes to rice. To much laughter from his followers, I replied that, on balance, we preferred potatoes. He smiled and then, staring at me with his piercing eyes and great seriousness, said that the Arabs preferred rice and that in my work with his Armed Forces and with him, I was to ensure that I gave **'Rice Solutions'** to him and not **'Potato Solutions'**.

In one short and very perceptive comment, the Chief had summed up the approach that we should take as we are setting out to work in the Gulf. We must never think that we have been brought in to a company or organization simply to impose our Western standards and principles on our Arab hosts because we may think that they are, of course, far better than anything that they possess. Some people have taken that approach and have had earlier return flights than they had expected!

What I present here is a **Rice Solution** to leadership and management, not the **Potato Solution** that may be more familiar to a European or North American audience. For ease, I will refer throughout to "Westerners". The Rice Solution can only be found once we understand as much as we can about the culture and characteristics of Gulf Arab people and to achieve this we have to read, listen, watch and discuss at every possible opportunity.

I will give you a few things to think about as you approach a job where you will be working closely with, or even for, Gulf Arab people, or simply planning a business trip to the region. It will also have relevance throughout the remainder of the Middle East and North Africa.

The Arabian Gulf region comprises the countries of Kuwait, Saudi Arabia, Qatar, the United Arab Emirates (UAE), Oman and Bahrain. It includes southern Iraq but not Iran, which has its own distinct culture and does not consider itself an Arab country. The countries of the Arabian Gulf, formerly known as 'the Persian Gulf' are all unique in their own ways with colourful histories as well as different economies and politics, but they all share the common values of being both Arab and Muslim. For the purposes of this book, I will refer to the Arabian Gulf region as 'the Gulf'.

This book will give you some pointers on what has been called 'the Gulf Arab leadership style' and it will illustrate a few methods that you might consider as you take your place in, or alongside, an organization owned, led or managed by Gulf Arab people. Here you will need to adapt to the Gulf style of leadership and management that is going to be most effective for the role you are undertaking.

I will talk a good deal about both leadership and management. So, for the purpose of this, let us agree the following descriptions of the two:

> **Leadership**: Leadership is the ability to influence and guide others in a common direction or towards a common goal, thereby enabling people to make decisions that leave them feeling empowered.

> **Management**: Management is the process of dealing with resources and people in order to achieve defined objectives. It is more about nurture than nature and can certainly be taught and practiced.

These are classic definitions but – in essence – the context of this book is simply about:

> communicating effectively with a group of people from various and very different backgrounds and cultures, motivating them, creating trust and forging them into an effective team that will deliver success.

It is not my intention to discuss the broader issues of nature over nurture although I believe that there is a large slice of nature in leadership: some people are naturally more gifted leaders than others. However, leadership can still be taught and nurtured and will develop with experience.

The question often arises as to whether or not one can be an excellent leader and a poor manager, or vice versa. I can think of one or two examples where inspirational leaders are sometimes not good managers. One of the most charismatic leaders I was lucky enough to work with in the British Army disliked anything to do with administration and spent little of his time engaged with it. As a result, his organization and his people suffered from a series of administrative challenges, to put it politely, but such was his inspirational leadership that he was adored and followed by all. In fairness to him, he identified his own weakness and filled the gap in his ability with high-performing assistants. This ability to know yourself and identify your weaker areas is an important but separate point altogether and worthy of greater discussion but not in this book.

The ideal model is where leadership and management combine equally and in harmony and, for the purposes of this guide, I will refer to the two as though they were an effective double act.

Now, having defined some terms, let us return to the main theme of the impending move or business trip to the region. As you consider your move, hopefully, you will have done some preparation for your role. For example, you will have:

- learned some useful Arabic phrases;

- familiarized yourself with some of the normal conventions;

- completed some general research about the culture and religion of the country you are about to work in; and

- carried out some due diligence on the company you will be working with.

I will not repeat too much of that here, but my first piece of advice is that if you have not already taken these simple steps, you should now. It will pay dividends and avoid some early embarrassments. There are many very good books on the market that will help you – see the 'Recommended Reading List' on p. 115.

My first experience working alongside people of the Islamic religion began in 1994 when I worked as a British Army Officer with the United Nations to support the Bosniak Muslims in the besieged enclave of Gorazde in what was known at the time as the Former Republic of Yugoslavia and is now part of Bosnia Herzegovina. The citizens and fighters in the town were Muslims but not Arabs, although shadowy figures often appeared to fight alongside the defenders who were said to be former Mujahadin fighters from many Arab countries. They had gained their experience of fighting in the earlier war in Afghanistan against the Soviet Army. This was my earliest exposure to the bond that exists between those of the Muslim faith.

Some years later, my relationship with the region began, originally as a British Army Officer working closely with Arab Armed Forces from across the Gulf and Levant and more recently in business working for a large multinational company under the ownership of an Arab family in Kuwait and then as CEO of a business operating throughout Saudi Arabia including the holy cities of Mecca and Medina, and in Bahrain.

Soon after leaving the Army, I joined a Company in Kuwait that was owned by two of the original trading families in the country. I witnessed almost as soon as I had joined them, a bitter family dispute which caused the business severe problems. Caught in the middle of this family dispute was an expatriate leadership team. I witnessed first-hand, leadership and management styles under severe pressure and the breaking down of team spirit that at the time, I was not fully prepared for. As we battled to extricate the business from terminal trouble, I had to draw on every element of my military experience and in particular my leadership training. I had to temper it, however, with a large dose of cultural understanding in order to identify what would work and what would simply not. These events reinforced my already strongly held view that a simple adherence to Western learned leadership and management principles will only be successful if it is combined with a solid understanding of all of the local cultural issues at play. The one without the other will be sub-optimal and may lead you to make poor business decisions.

This book is a critical appraisal of the differences between a Western approach to leadership and management and a Gulf Arab approach. At no stage do I intend to state that one style or the other is better or worse but rather to present the picture in a balanced way and to show how the cultures can work together and complement each other. If I have given offence to anyone by what might appear a too critical approach, then I apologize unreservedly. In all areas, I will offer possible Rice Solutions to situations.

I do not suggest for a moment that I have all the answers (and indeed nor could anyone brought up in the West), but my intention is to give you some 'food for thought' before you arrive in the job, and that this may help you to enjoy every moment of your forthcoming experience working with some of the most hospitable and generous people in the world.

As an example of why I think this is so important, I include a vignette that is based on the real experiences of several people:

Richard looked out of the window of his office at the

rain falling steadily on the rooftops of London. He thought of the late finish ahead of him, the long walk through the cold March rain to the station and the train trip that would take him home. The children would be in bed already and he would have just enough time to eat a reheated supper with his wife before falling into bed. He pressed "Send" on the letter of application for the treasury job with a multinational company based in the Arabian Gulf.

With his accountancy degree from a top UK university and his recently awarded MBA from a leading business school in the USA, he flew through the interview stage and was offered a five-day visit to the region with his wife to complete the final interview. With the business class flights and the luxurious hotel with the sea view, Richard and his wife thoroughly enjoyed their "second honeymoon". He took the job.

On arrival at the company, the family were shown to their villa and Richard quickly started work. He found that many of the processes and leadership styles were not as he had expected, and he felt a growing sense of unease about the job he had taken. It was extremely hot by now, the children's school was not due to start for several months, and the promised driving licence and car for his wife were mired in bureaucracy. The cockroach infestation in the kitchen was the final straw. Richard resigned during his probation period and the family headed back to the UK.

The company leadership smiled ruefully that another expatriate had failed to persevere and they advertised again for the post. The considerable financial waste for the advertising, recruitment and on-boarding process sparked some controversy but there was nothing that could have been done.

Or was there?

As part of the initial process and before any large financial outlay, a short familiarization course for Richard and his wife covering everything from leadership and management styles in the Gulf to an explanation of some of the domestic issues to expect, would have prepared Richard and his family for the experience as well as enabling them to opt out at an early stage. It would have been a cost-effective and vitally important early step in the recruitment process.

CHAPTER 2

Context – Some Religion and History

In order to give you the very best chance of making a success of your work in the Gulf, it is important that you have some knowledge of the following key subjects that will give you some important context:

- Islam, the religion.

- The history and spread of Islam.

- The historical Importance of the Gulf to the West.

There is a wide range of excellent books that you should read to give you a deeper understanding of these subjects – some quite high-brow, others "easy reads". Again, see the 'Recommended Reading List' on p. 115.

Let's start by looking at the key tenets of the Islamic religion.

Islam – The Religion

It is worth stressing that the culture in the Gulf is based primarily on the Islamic religion and the countries consider themselves to be Muslim countries and not secular as we are in the West. Raphael Patai, the Hungarian Jewish cultural anthropologist who wrote the controversial classic, *The Arab Mind*, states that 'Religion is not one aspect of life but the hub from which all else radiates.'

This is an important distinction because the religious mores and principles of Islam drive everything from laws to certain types of behaviour. The degree to which Islam permeates every facet of life, however, is different from country to country in the Gulf. Furthermore, the interpretations of Islam itself differ not only from country to country but in some cases even from mosque to mosque, which can complicate any attempt to gain a complete picture of the influences of Islam and the teachings of the Prophet Mohammed. A simple example of this is the attitude towards alcohol in the Gulf, which differs significantly from Saudi Arabia and Kuwait to Bahrain to United Arab Emirates (UAE) and Qatar.

Even if you, personally, have no belief in any God or any religion, it is still very important that you understand the religious influences at play in the Gulf. Arabs have a respect, however, for those who have a faith and they may not be impressed by anyone who strongly states an agnostic or atheist view. I strongly suggest that you keep this to yourself if this is the case.

I would suggest that, for many, our own understanding of Islam is heavily influenced by what we read or see in the press. It is true to say that, since the appalling events of 11 September 2001 and the actions of ISIS, the coverage has not always been positive and is rarely balanced. This leaves many of us with a view that Islam is a religion of Jihad, subjugation of women and discrimination against all other religions (particularly Christian and Judaism) and that the Qur'an is full of encouragement to fight and to die for the cause of Islam. Take this quote for example: 'Anyone arrogant enough to reject the verdict of the judge or of the priest who represents your God must be put to death.'

Bloodthirsty and anti-Christian? Certainly bloodthirsty but not anti-Christian, given that this is a quote from the Old Testament of the Bible.

I promise that I am not making a cheap religious point here: I use it rather to highlight the point that, if we are about to work in a country that is Islamic, then we must try and have at least a basic understanding of it and –

in particular – where it will have an impact on business practices such as leadership and management. Maybe, also, I would suggest that a deeper understanding of our own religion or beliefs is important if we are to pass judgement on Islam. But I am straying into polemic here and that is not my purpose.

The commonly held view of Islam by many throughout the world is often neither well informed nor correct. Islam is a complex and multifaceted religion and its title "Islam" simply means submission to God. The name of the Muslim God is Allah and you will often hear phrases mentioning Allah in regular conversation such as 'I am well, Alhumduli' Allah (Praise be to God)'.

Islam developed from around 600 AD when the Prophet Mohammed lived in the Western part of what is now Saudi Arabia. At the time, the Middle East region was divided between Christians, Jews and those who worshipped multiple Gods. I will talk more of the spread of Islam later in this chapter.

The religious culture is taken not only from the holy book, the Qur'an (or Koran) and the teachings of the Prophet Mohammed but also from the wider writings of his followers (or Sahabah, as they were known in Islam). These writings concern the behaviour and, more specifically, the reported sayings of the Prophet, known collectively as the Hadiths. This body of work heavily influences every facet of Gulf Arab culture including leadership and management. There are many schools and strands of Islam such as Sunni, Shia, Sufi and Wahabi, but all follow the same holy book.

In speech and writing in Islam, the words 'Peace be upon Him' or 'PBUH' are placed after any mention of the Prophet Mohammed. It would not be expected for non-

Muslims to do this, but you would not be wrong to do it. I have not done it in this book.

It is worth noting that the Islamic calendar is called the "Hijri Calendar". It is based on a lunar month and not synchronized with the Gregorian Calendar. As a result, key events such as Ramadan and Hajj, which I shall talk about later, shift dates every year. Government departments and their agencies often issue documents with Hijri dates, and it is important to have a date converter close to hand to avoid missing deadlines.

The Islamic religion is built on the **5 Pillars,** which every Muslim is required to follow strictly although, of course, some do not:

- **Profession of Faith (Shahada).** The basic creed of Islam is that: **There is no God but God and Mohammed is his messenger.** Muslims acknowledge that Christianity and Judaism are closely related and that Moses, Jesus Christ and Mohammed are all prophets for the same God. The three religions are termed "Abrahamic" religions because they all acknowledge the fundamental importance of the Prophet Abraham and consider him the father of their religions. It is interesting to note that the Islamic Holy Book, The Qur'an, mentions Moses, Abraham and Jesus more times than it does its own prophet, Mohammed. To a Muslim, Mohammed was the last and most recent prophet, born as he was in 570 AD and, therefore, his message is the latest and so the most relevant. Many Muslims are perplexed by the Christian's failure to understand that Mohammed was bringing an updated message from God.

- **Prayer (Salat).** Muslims are required to pray five times a day at set times. The first prayer for the most devout is extremely early as it coincides with sunrise. This point, combined with the afternoon heat in summer, is why school and working days often start early. Many of you, I am sure, will have woken up early on holidays or business trips to the call to prayer from the mosques. Very often, meetings will be organized around the prayer and do not be surprised if a Gulf Arab person excuses themself to pray. In some countries in the region, particularly Saudi Arabia, shops and restaurants closed during prayers time up until very recently A quick nip out at your lunch break to do a shop or grab a sandwich could be a hollow experience as a result.

- **Giving of Alms (Zakat).** Muslims are required to give a percentage of their wealth to the poor as charity. This can take the form of the donation of complete buildings such as mosques by the very wealthy to the offering of small amounts of cash or food to those less fortunate. The practice is particularly prevalent during Ramadan where you will see every traffic light intersection or garage forecourt being cleaned permanently as expatriate workers wait expectantly for cash to be passed out from waiting cars. You will also see tents set up throughout cities during Ramadan to feed those breaking their fast.

There are two aspects of Zakat that should be understood. Zakat has a personal commitment but, in most countries in the Gulf there is also a government-imposed Zakat tax on trade. This is administered differently throughout the region but, for example, in Saudi Arabia it takes the form of a 2.5% levy placed against the Retained Earnings of a Company. This is separate to the individuals' contribution.

The personal commitment to pay Zakat is unregulated and allows individuals to calculate their complete wealth including property, cars and even wives' jewelry, and then make a contribution direct to the poor or needy of the same 2.5%.

- **Fasting (Sawan).** Ramadan is the ninth month of the Islamic calendar and celebrates the month when the Qur'an was revealed to the Prophet Mohammed. Muslims are required to abstain from food, drink, cigarettes and sex during the hours of daylight. In many countries, it is illegal to break the fast in public although arrangements are often made to allow non-Muslims to eat in seclusion. Generally, Muslims look forward to this period as an opportunity to reconnect with their religion, and it is a period of active community and family life with people fasting, praying and socializing together. Work is not a primary concern for most and, as Ramadan progresses, the cumulative effects of lack of sleep and fasting can cause any workforce to lose some effectiveness, which should always be taken into account. Office hours are reduced during the period to ease the life of all those fulfilling Ramadan. It is also the case that big decisions are seldom made during this period and certainly important supporting work such as contract finalization can be slowed by the shorter working hours. There also tends to be a slowdown in business between Ramadan and the following Eid holiday although you may find clients or colleagues ringing you to discuss issues late into the night as they use their time between prayer and mealtimes.

- **Pilgrimage (Hajj).** Every Muslim is required to make one visit in their lifetime to visit the Ka'aba, the centre of the Haram Mosque in the Holy City of Mecca in Saudi Arabia. The Hajj take place in a ten-day period in the twelfth month of the Islamic calendar and around two million people gather to perform the rites together. The rituals include dressing in a simple white garment and walking in circles around the Ka'aba. Special leave is granted to people to allow them to complete the Hajj. Many people will take part in a religious visit to Mecca at other times and this is known as "Umrah". Completion of Umrah is viewed very highly in Islam. It will gain the individual favour on the final day of atonement, but it does not count as completing the Hajj.

Islam has several vital underpinning beliefs that form the foundation of the religion. Many of these are shared by the other Abrahamic religions. These beliefs are known as the **"Six Articles of Faith or Iman"** and they are clearly laid out in the Qur'an:

- Belief in the existence and oneness of God.
- Belief in the existence of Angels.
- Belief in the existence of the books that came from God or Allah: Qur'an; Gospels; Torah and the Psalms.
- Belief in the Prophets of which Jesus is one and Mohammed is the most recent.
- Belief in a Day of Judgement.
- God's Predestination.

No book about working and leading in the Gulf would be complete without a mention of the topic of **Shariah or**

Islamic Law. It is a much misunderstood subject and often misconstrued, sometimes deliberately for political reasons. "Shariah" simply means "path" and is derived from the Holy Qur'an and the Hadiths. It provides personal religious law and moral guidance and, although it underpins the Law, it is not in itself a set of rules adjudicated in court. It is, however, extremely conservative. It is interesting to note that there are many similarities between the Shariah Law and the way law is practiced in Europe and the UK. My advice is to have a clear understanding of its effect in whichever country in the Gulf you are working in and, above all, to be sensible. It is always extremely disappointing to hear examples of expatriates arrested or fined in some of the more liberal countries in the Gulf such as UAE for behaviour that demonstrates a complete lack of respect for the mores of Islam and a fundamental misunderstanding of the Islamic Law of the country. Shariah also underpins the banking practices in the region and it is important, if you are working with local banks, that you have a good understanding of the areas where this will have an impact on your business. For example, there is no interest on bank loans because that is not permitted under Shariah and, therefore, banks charge for loans in different ways.

Islam – The History

Islam is still the fastest growing religion in the world. There are currently approximately two billion Muslims spread across the world and it is the dominant religion in 50 countries. The spread of Islam began in approximately 610 AD when the Prophet Mohammed and his followers began the process of converting the people of Arabia from the worship of many Gods to the Islamic faith.

Initially, Islam was spread by military raids throughout Arabia until the death of the Prophet in 633 AD. In 634 AD, an Arab and Muslim Army under the leadership of what became known as "the Caliphs" began the determined process of spreading Islam in all directions. By 713 AD, a mere hundred years after the death of the Prophet Mohammed, despite the schism that had created the Sunni and Shia factions, an Islamic empire dominated from as far as Spain and Portugal (and small parts of Southern France) in the West to India and Pakistan in the East. Most Muslims believe that the Muslim leaders in the occupied countries were benign rulers and allowed freedom of religion although they did require the payment of a tax to secure this freedom. In some countries, Jews and Christians were even considered Protected Persons. Many locals, particularly the wealthy, converted to Islam as a means of finding favour with their Muslim overlords and the roots of the Islamic religion spread as a result.

Although the spread of Islam was completed mostly through military occupation through Arabia and North Africa, a large expansion came about through trade, particularly along the Silk Road, the trade route that ran from China through India, Persia (modern-day Iran) and into Europe. Many wealthy Muslim merchants set up staging posts and made their homes along the route. There are many superb examples along the Silk Road of mosques and Islamic rest houses where travelling traders were able to find food and rest. The spread of Islam to the Far East was completed mainly through the same peaceful trade.

This vast Islamic Empire entered what is known as the "Golden Age" between the 8th and 13th centuries. The Empire took the teachings of the Qur'an and its encouragement for knowledge, and led the way particularly in the areas of science, commerce and medicine. Many Greek books were translated into Arabic and subsequently Latin. leading to the dissemination of "lost" ancient knowledge across the Empire and into Western Europe. It is interesting to note that, at the same time that the Islamic world was enjoying a wonderful period of innovation and development, Europe was in the period known as the "Dark Ages".

The Islamic Empire ended abruptly in 1258 with the invasion by the Mongol hordes from the North led by Genghis Khan. In 1492, the Empire also lost both Spain and Portugal. For the next few centuries, the Caliphates reduced in influence and power, but they had left a strong Islamic footprint behind them in the countries that they had previously occupied.

Arabian Gulf – Importance to UK and the West

Why is the region important to the West and – indeed – why are you or your company there at all?

It is unlikely to be for the scenery, which for large parts can be rather flat and featureless, although in several of the Arabian Gulf countries there are wonderful and relatively undiscovered spaces; the weather that is either blisteringly hot or energy-sapping humid; or the ease of doing business because it can be incredibly bureaucratic; or the relaxed political situation that can be autocratic and opaque at best.

Is it, therefore, just the fact that you receive a tax-free salary? I think it is deeper than that, although that is, of course, extremely attractive. The joint history between the West and the Gulf, and the respect in which Western business practices and experience are still held, mean that the Gulf remains an exciting place to work and do business. Expatriate Westerners with their knowledge and experience of operating in the West are still considered a valuable asset.

There are many large multinational companies operating throughout the Gulf that are led and managed on Western lines with many high-quality expatriate managers in senior positions or working as consultants.

In the next decade, however, our attractiveness will reduce as Arabization increases due to falling oil prices and demand and – with it – the requirement to diversify the economy, reduce the number of local people working in the public sector, and minimize the amount of government welfare benefits. It is interesting to note that, during the coronavirus pandemic in Saudi Arabia, the Saudi Government was very quick to raise taxes and to reduce welfare payments as a measure to fund the assistance measures for the economy. These measures not only had an impact on the expatriate community but also on the Saudi nationals.

To understand the historic importance of the Gulf to the West and the UK particularly, you simply need to lay a ruler down on a map between India and the UK and see where it falls. The line passes straight up the Arabian Gulf.

From as early as the 16th century, the UK was developing its interest in India and a trade route was required from the Indian subcontinent up to the mother country. The land routes were too long and too difficult to protect; there was a route around the Cape of Good Hope in Africa, but it was not only an extremely dangerous route: it also took many months. The UK therefore started establishing trading posts in all the countries up the Gulf with one of the first being placed in Persia as early as 1622. Trade was taken up the Gulf to what is now Kuwait and Southern Iraq, and then cross loaded onto camel trains and taken across the land to the Mediterranean on trade routes that had been used for thousands of years. One of the oldest buildings in Kuwait today is the former post office set up by the British where mail from British India was sorted and dispatched across the desert.

For many centuries, the UK developed alliances and treaties with all the local tribal leaders along the length of the Gulf to trade for their valuable pearls and to seek protection for their convoys as they plied their trade in their waters. The British dominated the area and, of course, played a major part in the establishment of the countries that we now know as Iraq, Iran, UAE, Kuwait, Bahrain, Qatar and Saudi Arabia. It is true to say that, for many centuries, nothing happened within the region without British involvement and leadership. There is an old saying in Iraq that: 'If there are two fish fighting in the Euphrates, the British will be behind them somewhere.'

This is a fascinating period of history with so many twists and turns that this short synopsis cannot do justice to. There are so many excellent books and documentaries on the subject.

This British involvement has left an indelible mark on all the countries in the region.

The situation changed in 1869, however, when the Suez Canal was opened and, although initially it was too shallow to take large trade vessels, by 1875 it had been developed into the main trade route from the Indian sub-continent to the UK. In the next 50 years, the pearl trade collapsed due to the Depression and the production of cultured pearls by the Japanese, and the region became less important to the UK. After the First World War, there was a further significant reorganization of treaties and alliances, and even countries within the Gulf as the Ottoman Empire was broken up, mostly between the UK and France.

In 1947, India received its independence and Pakistan was created. The role of the British in India was consequently over and, with it, the need to enable trade throughout the Gulf.

Oil was discovered early in the 20th century by the UK (although its presence is mentioned in the Qur'an) but it was not until 1930 that the first commercially viable fields were discovered in Saudi Arabia. During the next 20 years, hugely profitable oil fields were opened in all countries of the Arabian Gulf although the Second World War slowed the development.

The discovery and development of oil in the Gulf is arguably one of the most formative events in the region's history. The period saw untold wealth arriving in a period of a few years. This development of instant wealth is not considered to be altogether positive, however. Various phrases have been used to explain the situation that the Gulf faced from **The Paradox of Plenty** or the **Resource Curse**. The conclusion is that the countries of the region faced less economic growth because they relied on one asset, developed with less democracy and their economies did not diversify. As part of my research for this book, I spent many hours discussing the history of the Gulf with a Kuwaiti who ran a business school. She referred to the arrival of oil in Kuwait as the start of **The Age of Spoiling**. She went on to explain that the distribution of the oil wealth had created a generation of young men and women throughout the Gulf who expected large financial handouts at every stage, were not prepared to work hard for a living, were inherently lazy and had no sense of social conscience. She lamented the loss of the noble Arab virtues caused by the free distribution of oil wealth.

The situation in the Gulf changed dramatically in 1968 when the UK Government declared that the UK would withdraw completely from the region by 1971 in a policy that became known as "East of Suez". Although it is acknowledged that the decision was made mostly on economic grounds as a cost-saving exercise, it also fitted with the overall withdrawal from Empire process that had started after the end of the Second World War. It is important to note, however, that the Gulf countries were not formally part of the British Empire: they were considered protectorates but were never constitutional colonies. The decision to withdraw was not popular in the region as Gulf countries feared for their security in the uncertain world that developed after the Suez Crisis of 1956 and the growing Arab nationalism that spread after the event. Several countries led by Kuwait asked the UK to remain and declared that they would be willing to pay for the security, but this was not accepted by the UK Government because it was believed that the British Forces would become little less than mercenaries. As a result of the close relationships forged at the time, there are enduring good relationships between the UK and the Gulf rulers. By 1971, however, Bahrain, Qatar and UAE were fully independent from the UK.

The combined effects of the coronavirus pandemic and an evolution in the oil industry, whereby output will become far greater than demand and countries are already being forced to innovate and develop in areas other than oil and gas, will have long-term consequences in the Gulf that will affect many areas. It will be fascinating to see over the next decades whether the pandemic and the loss of demand for oil and gas marks a new age of enlightenment and change.

CHAPTER 3

Adopting
the Right Mindset

> Yesterday, I was clever so I wanted to change the world.
> Today, I am wise so I am changing myself.
> – Jalal ad Din Muhammed Rumi (1207–1273)

I mentioned in Chapter I that it is a very good idea to do some preliminary reading before you arrive in your new appointment or business trip and there is an enormous amount that has been written on Arab and indeed Islamic culture over the years (Remember the 'Recommended Reading List' on p. 115.)

There are several examples of people in history who have worked alongside the Arabs, embraced their culture and achieved significant results. Although it is difficult to fully separate the fact from the romantic fiction that grew up around one of these, Colonel T.E. Lawrence, or "Lawrence of Arabia" as he became known after the First World War, is one of the most noteworthy.

T.E. Lawrence. Lawrence joined the British Army at the outbreak of the War and was posted to Egypt. He had previously learned the Arab language and culture as an archeologist in the Gulf and so was posted to the Intelligence branch of the Army as a liaison officer between the British and the Arab Forces under Sharif Hussein, the Emir of the Holy City of Mecca. At the time, the British were attempting to encourage an Arab revolt against their Ottoman (Turkish) overlords throughout the Middle East. Turkey had joined the Germans, and the British plan was to keep them focused in the region so that they could not reinforce their German allies. From 1916 to 1918, Lawrence worked alongside the Arabs and, in particular, Hussein's son, Emir Faisal, advising, training and leading several daring raids against the Ottoman Turks. His exploits are captured in his autobiography, *The Seven*

Pillars of Wisdom. In 1917, he was commissioned by the British Army to write a pamphlet on leadership among the Bedouin Arabs. He was working many years before oil had been discovered in the Gulf and the Arabs, generally, led a life that was uncomplicated by vast wealth and Western influences. Also, of course, he was working alongside the Arabs at a time of conflict, as they battled to rid themselves of the Ottoman Turk. Despite all this, he was a man who learned to understand the Arabs intimately and many of his Articles stand the test of time and provide much to think about today. He published his 27 Articles in the *Arab Bulletin* in August 1917.

One of the Articles that is particularly relevant, and which I refer to on an almost daily basis, deals with the frustrations that we can feel when dealing with people brought-up in a different culture. Of course, we can get a little frustrated at times working in the Gulf and, indeed, Lawrence did on occasions but the following statement from him is worth considering: 'Better the Arabs do it tolerably than you do it perfectly. It is their war and you are to help them, not to win it for them.'

And so, our first step must be to accept that there will be differences in approach and to look for ways of accommodating them, if not even celebrating them. You may want a 100% solution to a particular issue or challenge but that may be because you are trying to find the Potato Solution: remember that we are striving for the Rice Solution.

The Grain

Gulf Arab people were trading people, and the skill of boat building was an important one as their dhows plied their trade through some of the most difficult and treacherous waters as they pushed further and further East in search of new markets. Their crews worked with the constant threat not only of sudden squalls and difficult tides such as around the Strait of Hormuz, the narrow pass between modern-day Iran and Oman, but also of pirates who roamed freely along the coasts looking for ships to pillage. Dhow building was a great skill passed down from father to son, and the dhow builders knew that the only way to work with wood to achieve the correct shape and size was to identify the grain of the wood and to work with it and not across it. Working across the grain would only result in that piece of wood breaking or your being in receipt of several painful splinters.

The Arab culture is as embedded in the national character as the grain is in a piece of wood. We therefore need to identify the **Grain of the Wood**, and then be prepared to work with it and bend it in the direction we wish it to go, not to plane across it.

So, first, I would suggest that we must understand the people culture, particularly the leadership and management culture (or the **grain**), and then look for solutions that will allow us to work with it to achieve our aims. Accommodate it, do not fight it, although there may be times – as in any business environment worldwide – when you are left with only one option and that is to stop and start again. This will all take time and patience. At times, you will make mistakes but do not be put off by this: just keep trying.

I once took a box of chocolates to my neighbour's house in Kuwait to wish him a happy Eid Al Fitr holiday at the end of Ramadan. I was escorted by my three children. We entered the house and were shown into the family meeting-room, or Diwan, where I was surprised to see around 50 solemn-looking men sitting around the room. I shook hands with everyone and eventually greeted my host and passed over the chocolates with a jolly 'Eid Mubarak'. As I turned to leave, the eldest son stood up and escorted me out explaining that, although I was very welcome, his father's father had died the night before and I had visited a Condolence ceremony where the family friends and relations had gathered to show their respect to the dead man. I had failed to read that chapter in the culture guide dealing with the Arab practice of Condolence. It was extremely embarrassing at the time although the hospitality of Gulf Arab people is such that they were very touched by the gesture and saw the funny side immediately. However, my three daughters who came with me have not yet forgiven me, several years later. My neighbour and I have remained firm friends since; my daughters still cringe at the thought!

Before I completely confuse you with metaphors, I would use one more and that is that at all times we should try and view every issue or challenge through the optic of the Gulf Arab person and be prepared to turn our own "telescope" around and look at the problem through the other end: the Arab end. To do that, of course, we must take the time and use our intelligence to understand the influences that give Gulf Arab people this perspective. As an example of this, when I took over my first job out of the Army in Kuwait with one of the trading families, I was responsible for delivering an important logistics project against some tight deadlines. I was insistent with my mostly Arab team that timings were important and that, if I asked for a meeting at a particular time it meant that time and not many minutes later. At one point, one of my Kuwaiti staff said to me in exasperation, 'Why do you have to over-complicate things with these detailed timings?'

I had assumed that everyone would understand that sticking to good timing allowed for better planning and avoided complexity. I had not appreciated that this approach was seen as an additional complexity by my Arab colleagues. I was rather taken aback but could only laugh as I realized how my insistence had been interpreted.

At all times, it is important, however, that we do not lose sight of either our aim or our own leadership and management principles and standards. One of the greatest insults that could be levelled against officers serving with the Indian Army or the Indian Civil Service during the period of British India was for them to be accused of having gone native (a term that would not be used today). This was a pejorative description of an officer or official who may have adopted the dress, style and culture of the local Indians and indeed, disgrace of disgraces, possibly taken an Indian wife or mistress. We must decide how **native** we are prepared to go with our leadership and management. What are the issues that we are not prepared to compromise on, and what are the issues that we are prepared to give ground on? We should adapt our style to fit the environment and perhaps the circumstance. The degree of adaptation is a decision that only you can make, however. This relates back directly to Lawrence of Arabia's 27 Articles and the advice to follow the "Arab Way". Try and identify your red lines or, in other words, standards that you will not compromise on. I once met up with the CEO of a large luxury car franchise in Kuwait who was retiring early although after 20 years with the same family business. I asked him why he was leaving, and he commented that he had shifted his red lines so often over the years that finally it had come to the point where he felt he could make no further adjustments and he had to leave.

In summary, but as an important starting point, as we wait at the airport ready to fly towards our new post or a business meeting, we should make the decision that we are going to arrive at the other end with the right mindset – one that will allow us to look, listen and learn; to embrace the local culture; and to be prepared to alter our own methods rather than remaining 'fixed'. At all times, we must strive to gain knowledge. I would suggest that in dealings with Gulf Arab people there has seldom been more truth in the old saying that **'God gave you two ears and one mouth for a reason**...' We should use them in that ratio.

Remember; understand the grain; view situations through an Arab optic; and – finally – strive at all times to look for the Rice Solution.

CHAPTER 4

Leadership and Islam

First Principles

It is important as a starting point to look at some of the similarities and differences between our own Western principles of leadership and management and those of the Islamic religion so that we can quickly identify areas in common and those where there is a divergence.

Some might say that leadership and management as we understand them are, themselves, Western concepts, and they are neither well understood nor accepted by Gulf Arab people who are happier seeking group decisions and not deferring to a single individual. The great Gulf Arab tradition of the menfolk particularly, but not exclusively, meeting together to discuss every issue and seeking agreement is still very much in evidence today. Known as **"Diwanyah"** or **"Majlis"**, depending on which Gulf country you are in, issues are discussed and group solutions sought. Notwithstanding this, I would suggest that the contrary is actually true, and that Gulf Arab people are happy with a mixture of the two approaches. (The Arabic words mean "guest room" or "meeting room" and have given their names to the practice of meeting together, similar to the use of the word "salon" in French.)

The Prophet Mohammed was tested as a leader in both peace and war as he sought to spread the word of Islam throughout the Arab world. From his earliest days as a shepherd, when he had already achieved a reputation for wisdom and integrity, to his leading his forces successfully to victory at the battle of Badr, he understood fully the need for leadership in any task, even the most menial, and he provides many examples of unequivocal support for its importance – for instance, 'When travelling on a journey, even if there are only three of you, make one a leader' (Source: Hadiths. Abu Dawn)

Trying to encapsulate something such as leadership, which is so intangible, into one single abiding principle is difficult. In our Western culture, however, it is hard to find a better example of a simple phrase that encapsulates the essence of good leadership than the one which is found in the motto of the British Army's Royal Military Academy of Sandhurst where generations of British Army Officers and, indeed, officers from many other nations including the Arabian Gulf, have been trained: **Serve to Lead**.

This apparent contradiction explains the requirement for every leader to have at their core the needs and welfare of the team: the workforce. This is not in a subservient way but in the sense that the leader understands the needs of the group, the team and the individuals, and places those before themself and their own needs. This is sometimes referred to as the **Servant Leader Concept**. Dr John Adair, the acknowledged first Professor of Leadership and former officer of the renowned Arab Legion, encapsulates this in his Three Circles of Needs (see Figure 4.1), which many of you may be familiar with through your own leadership training. He has also written of his experiences working with the Arab Legion in the 1940s and the Arabs' approach to leadership. Adair is a fascinating man and I was fortunate enough to meet him while researching this book. He worked under the renowned British Commander, General John Glubb, known by the Arabs as Glubb Pasha, who commanded the Arab Legion of Jordan (formerly Trans Jordan) and had considerable experience in the fighting against the newly formed state of Israel. His intimate knowledge of the Arab people and his experience of leadership, commanding Arab soldiers. make him, in my opinion, a greater source of relevant knowledge than T.E. Lawrence.

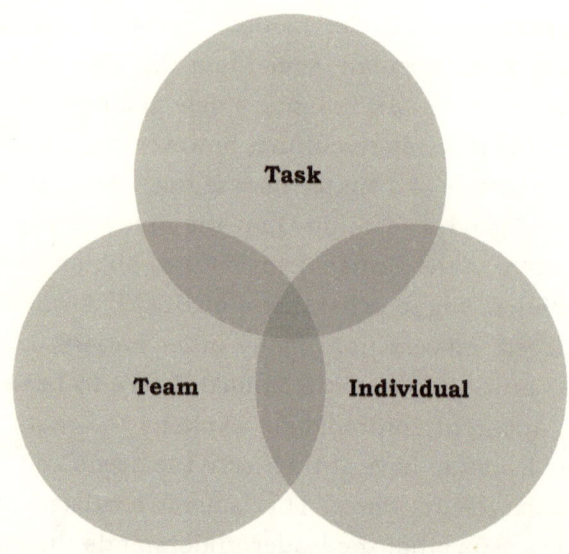

Figure 4.1 John Adair 'The Three Circles of Leadership Need'

The Three Circles of Needs is not simply a military approach to leadership: the same maxim is found throughout the commercial world. I worked for a period as a leadership consultant for a large private hospital chain in the UK and they had a similar creed: **'We are above all the agents of our people.'**

There are many examples from the life of the Prophet Mohammed where he displayed exactly this quality, and he reinforced this by stating: **'On a journey, the Lord of the people is their servant.'**

However, this simple concept, despite being clearly articulated by the Prophet, is not always well understood or even accepted by some Gulf Arab leaders and this is a clear example of where the principles of Islam do not necessarily sit comfortably with Arab culture. When I was assisting the Commandant of the Ali Al Sabah Military College, the initial officer training academy in Kuwait, with a handbook on leadership, a senior retired Kuwaiti naval officer who had agreed to act as my mentor throughout this work, laughed when I showed it to him and commented that the version that a few of the more "spoiled and entitled" military leaders would understand and be more comfortable with should read: 'I lead, therefore I should be served.' He went on to say, however, that servant leadership was deeply engrained in the tribal leaders of old.

You might suggest that it is a little cynical of my mentor, but it is a pointer towards the understanding of some of the cornerstones of good leadership that we will naturally understand and how they are interpreted by others in the region. It also highlights how **The Age of Spoiling**, which I talked of earlier, has had an adverse effect on the attitude to leadership of a minority of rich and privileged Gulf Arab people. The issue is that anything that even hints at subservience will not be readily accepted, even though the Prophet Mohammed encouraged people to be modest and self-effacing: **'Modesty is a part of Iman and Iman shall be rewarded with Paradise.'**

The lack of modesty and understanding of the Servant Leadership principle can manifest itself in what I would term a **"petit fonctionnaire"** mentality among some officials and those given responsibility over others. It is a mentality that can be extremely frustrating and unpleasant if the power is wielded in an unhelpful and unfriendly manner. Although it is slowly diminishing, it often appears with a small number of border officials or security staff who seem unaware of the adverse effect that their behaviour can have on visitors to their country. In business terms, for example, it can manifest itself in petty point-scoring against service providers by those charged with supervising contracts.

Supporting Behaviour

A strong set of values, or what the Arab may refer to as **"Noble Essence"**, must be the bedrock for any leadership style. Importantly, the values must be lived all the time. They are not part of a cloak that is put on when strong leadership is required – they must become part of the DNA or **grain** of any leader.

The British Army refers to them as the "Values and Standards": **Integrity, Discipline, Respect for Others, Courage, Loyalty and Selfless Commitment.** They apply to every leader at every level – both officers and non-commissioned officers – and their observance is taken extremely seriously.

The US Army has the same values but have formed them into a concise and easily remembered mnemonic:

- L – Loyalty
- D – Duty
- R – Respect
- S – Selfless Service
- H – Honor
- I – Integrity
- P – Personal Courage

I make no apologies for my military references because there is much that business has learned and can learn from the way the military approach leadership and management. The military is the only organization that requires its leaders to have an ability to ask its people to potentially make the ultimate sacrifice by putting themselves in harm's way. It is not a coincidence, therefore, that the military doctrine of leadership and management, which has been extremely well developed and tested in the harshest conditions, has been adopted by many successful businesses and organizations. The military are also very open to learning from other civilian organizations and they do. Consequently, their leadership and management principles and practices are a strong distillation of best practice.

This values-based leadership is certainly not the sole domain of the military, of course. Indeed, the same private medical business that I consulted for referred to their values and standards as their **Behaviours: Passion, Resilience, Disruption, Agility, Humanity and Partnership.**

Again, such values are not a Western invention: the Prophet Mohammed also understood the importance of strong values underpinning leadership: he was reported to have said: 'Whenever God makes a man responsible for other people, whether in greater or lesser numbers, he will be questioned as to whether he ruled his charges in accordance with God's decrees or not.' (Source: Hadiths. Ibn Hanbal)

There is no simple and single list of values in Islam but rather constant references and direction as to how people should lead their lives. However, the following list taken from the Hadiths does provide an example of a simple guide:

> **I will stand surety for Paradise if you save yourself from six things: Telling untruths; Violating promises; Dishonouring trust; Being unchaste in thought and act; Striking the first blow; Doing what is bad and unlawful.**

As an expatriate employee or business visitor, your

Arab host will expect you to have integrity and honesty, and they will not condone poor personal behaviour. Once you have gained their trust, there is much you will be able to achieve, although this may take some time. A breach of these simple principles can cause a major loss of trust and once lost, it will be impossible to regain it.

It appears, therefore, with the few examples that I have given, that leadership is the same the world over and Kuwaiti or British, Omani or American, we all share and understand the same basic principles and are able to apply them in any business setting.

However, I think there may be dragons on that path because there are other stronger influences at play which we need to be aware of and which I shall now discuss.

CHAPTER 5

Gulf Arab Culture in Business

One assumption that we all make at one stage or another is to believe that Islamic culture and Arab culture are one and the same thing. Everything that I read, and indeed witness, leads me to believe that this is not the case. In fact, it can be a dangerous assumption to consider that the two are the same. Such an assumption can lead us to expect one course of action from our Arab colleagues when actually the opposite plays out. We must, therefore, take time to understand the local Arab culture, which will be different from region to region within the Gulf, and to try and work out which is the dominant one at play in any situation: Islamic or Arab. At its worst, the tension between Islam and Arab can lead to behaviour that may be considered hypocritical in the West. This is not always easy to understand, and again will take time and a good deal of patience. What do I mean by this?

Many countries along the Arabian Gulf began their lives as small villages that made a living from fish and often pearl diving. The fish was mostly for their own consumption but they realized that they could earn significant wealth through selling their pearls. Several towns, therefore, developed as trading posts and every family was involved in some way in plying their trade down the Arabian Gulf, down the East African coast and across to the Indian subcontinent and beyond. Over many years, their wealth grew and the villages became walled cities, families intermarried and workers were brought in from across the seas to do the more manual jobs, thereby allowing the biggest families to establish themselves as wealthy trading families: a term still used today to describe the leading families in several countries. The traits of the trader were in place many years before the Islamic religion reached this distant part of what was then known as Arabia. Strongly in the DNA of many Gulf Arab people even today, therefore, is the ingrained mindset of the trader, an approach that always asks the question: 'What is in this for me?' In leadership terms, this leads them to a transactional style whereby stick and carrot are used to effect and achieving the aim is often only done through the offering of inducements, which is very evident in the workplace. This transactional approach has its roots deep in the local Arab culture. I would not consider it to be Islamic because it does not fit with the teachings of the Prophet, but it is Gulf Arab: regional and national.

Cultural Characteristics

There are several Arab cultural characteristics that will be present in the people in any organization and, unless you are prepared for them, they may appear strange. They are, however, engrained in the DNA and, if you are going to achieve the most from your employees or colleagues, you must understand them first and then attempt to work with them. This is the grain of wood that I spoke of earlier. I am not at all suggesting that 'working with' means that you should drop your own principles of leadership and management and completely adopt the mores and values of the country you are working in. I am saying, however, that you should understand your employers or colleagues and look for ways to work with them.

Remember, as I have said earlier, try and view issues not only through your own telescope but by being prepared to turn the telescope around and look at the problem through an Arabic optic – it may appear very different. Before I explain this, I must mention one important point that is what I refer to as the **cultural tension** that exists within most Gulf Arab people.

As previously discussed, Islam is the bedrock of the culture of the Gulf and it is extremely strong in people's attitude to tradition. The central belief is that the word that was given to the Prophet Mohammed directly from God cannot be changed or updated by mere mortals. This leads to a religion in which it can be perceived that old is good and new is potentially bad. Islam, however, started to spread its beliefs throughout the world in the 7th century AD but the Arab culture was developed over several thousand years before that. Many of the characteristics that make up the grain inevitably, therefore, come from Arabic and not necessarily Islamic roots. So, there is a potential tension between Islamic and pure Arabic cultures. This could be reasonably easy to decipher, were it not for the presence of another huge influence – that of Westernization.

Increasingly, Gulf Arab people are educated in the West, work with Western leaders at home and abroad, and are bombarded on all forms of media by Western ideals and mores. There is a significant increase throughout the region of Western business schools and universities opening to provide certificates and qualifications. Many Arabs even learn their English from television programmes and films from the USA and UK.

This all leads to the cultural tension whereby these three main influencers – Islam, Arabic Culture and Westernization – strive for preeminence. It can, I am certain, be difficult for Gulf Arab people (and extremely difficult for us) to determine which is the predominant influence but we need to be aware of them all.

Let us now look at some of the characteristics of the grain

and consider their impact on leadership and management:

Tribal and Family Loyalty. Loyalty to the tribe or family is one of the strongest characteristics of Gulf Arab people. It is forged in history from the time when the desert tribes lived together in tight communities and plundered other tribes for livestock and water, and, often, women as this old Bedouin maxim expresses: 'I and my brothers against my cousin; I and my cousins against the stranger.'

This loyalty will override any other loyalties and may require individuals to conform in any dispute, especially if the dispute is with another family or tribe. It can often result in family members showing favouritism to others of the same family and this is often done without anyone thinking that this is odd or unfair. Indeed, in the Arab mind, it would be extremely odd not to behave in this way. In those Gulf Arab countries that practice some form of political democracy, this loyalty to the family can act as a hindrance to complete freedom of choice for any individual to vote as they wish.

For example, you may have a business owner's son working in a company with you who may not be performing as you would want or expect, and this can be extremely challenging to manage. Think very carefully before you make a direct challenge against a family member that may put you in direct conflict with the Owners or Directors in case you enter into the dark world of family loyalty and **loss of face**, which I will discuss later.

On one occasion in Saudi Arabia, the local client's representative in a remote part of the Northern Provinces saw our company operation as an opportunity to provide employment for members of his extended family. Pressure was brought on one of my local managers to employ certain people who were without the right qualifications and experience, and our failure to comply caused frictions at a local level that we had to work hard to overcome. It was a constant source of tension between the client and my company. What surprised me was that the pressure to comply was not only tolerated by the client's Head Office staff, but it was also considered entirely normal and very much my issue to resolve.

Another aspect of this family loyalty is the exalted position of the elder in the tribe. The opinion of the older generation is given significant place in all discussions and issues, and the input from a 'grey beard' as they are called is often sought. In some companies, older statesmen may still come to work and enjoy the respect of the workforce despite their direct value to the business being slight or negligible. This is less likely in a large multinational company.

Dispute resolution. Linked with the previous paragraph, one important area where Arab culture plays a critical role concerns dispute – or even conflict resolution. In Arab culture, dispute is considered negative, disruptive and possibly even dangerous in the business setting. This is at odds with the Western view, which sees conflict in a business and the measures taken to solve it as a potentially positive part of the process of change. The word for dispute resolution in Arabia is **Sulha**, which has its roots in the Arabic word for peace, **Salaam**. The process of resolving conflict or dispute is, therefore, driven by the need to maintain peace and to ensure that all parties are satisfied with an honourable outcome. In the modern commercial setting, Arabs will often look to third-party intervention from a trusted and wise senior tribal member to solve disputes. All sides accept that there will be compromise and the final decision of the trusted elder is taken very seriously in order to maintain accord. In more serious civil cases – for example, where a crime such as murder has been committed – the process will also include the payment of 'blood money' from the family of the accused to the family of the victim. This ancient practice remains today in many parts of the region, and I witnessed it myself after a tragic accident on an Army exercise resulted in the death of a Kuwaiti Army officer. It was interesting to note at the time that the two other officers badly injured in the same accident, one from Oman and one from UK, received nothing and were not even considered in the resolution process.

Wasta or **Wasitah.** Known by other names in different parts of the Gulf, this is essentially nepotism or clout – or, to use an English expression, '**You scratch my back and I will scratch yours.**' It is a card that is played regularly and without any sense of shame. It is often allied to tribal or family loyalty but may extend to friends and business colleagues. An individual's Wasta may be based on simple authority achieved through their rank, their ability to be able to assist with friends and family or members of their tribe or country, if abroad, or their status within their religion. It will be used to help or gain favour or advantage in any situation. It can be a force for good but, if not controlled or if used for purely selfish motives, it can be extremely damaging to a team's morale and cohesion. An example often seen is selection for advancement or promotion that is sometimes done through Wasta and not given to the most deserving individual.

One of the jobs I was required to complete as an advisor to a Gulf Arab Ministry of Defence was to assist in the selection of students to attend professional military courses in the UK. On occasions, and despite my best efforts and advice to the contrary, the people selected for the most prestigious of courses were often those with the most Wasta. This sometimes left those more deserving and more professional feeling undervalued and even cheated – a leadership challenge in itself.

Wasta can, however, be worked to great advantage to ease your path through the Byzantine bureaucracy that you will face in your dealings with various ministries as you settle into a country in the Gulf. When my children arrived in Kuwait on their first visit and we discovered that their visas had run out the day before, a quick telephone call to a Kuwaiti official whom we had met previously resulted in extensions being instantly granted – a procedure that would have taken several weeks had we had to resort to officialdom.

In line with the transactional nature of Gulf Arab people, however, one should remember that a favour asked is a favour owed. Help or assistance will be freely given but there is an expectation that at some stage it will be repaid. Do not be surprised when this moment arrives.

There is also an expectation that, if you have some form of Wasta, you will play it, and being thoroughly Western and reserved about it is considered stupid at best and downright rude at worst. I was once doing some security consultancy for a large telecommunications company in the Gulf and a particular project was not developing as I would have liked. By coincidence, one of my wife's private patients (she is in the medical profession) was a Board member of this particular company and, when he discovered that I had been having problems with the project in his company, he made it very clear, through an associate of his, to my wife that I had insulted him by not seeking his assistance, his Wasta. Completely unknown to me, I had managed to alienate a member of the very Board that I was attempting to influence professionally.

Wasta is again part of the grain and any attempt to ignore it will prove fruitless. The key is to understand it first and then to try and minimize its adverse effects – often easier said than done. If your business processes are too reliant on the deployment of Wasta, it may be time to reappraise your strategies. Many Arabs will agree that its effect can be damaging, but they are mostly those who do not have it or who have suffered as a result of someone deploying it over them.

Wasta in its most extreme form is closely allied with corruption and money may pass hands in order to secure it in a particular situation. Many countries, within the Gulf and led by Saudi Arabia, have moved quickly to eradicate this at every level and one example is the introduction of online E-Forms for all Government Ministry business. This simple expedient has drastically reduced the effects of Wasta because it has removed the requirement for the companies' Government Relations Officers to interface personally with the Ministries in order to get business done.

Although the situation is slowly changing throughout the Gulf, there are still officials with the old mindset who see nothing wrong with Wasta gained in this way.

In many countries of the Gulf, Government initiatives to modernize and develop still have to permeate through a layer of long-held views that can act as a type of filter for new ideas. It can be frustrating because we can clearly see and applaud the overarching attempt to move forward in a modern way.

God's Will. You will frequently hear the expression '**Insh'allah**' in every walk of life. The term can be translated as, '**If it is God's Will, it will be done.**' It is a central belief in Islam that the fate of man is "maktub", written or predestined and that there is nothing that a human being can do to change their ultimate end or the events of their life.

According to the Qur'an, the utterance of Insh'allah must be made for any plan in the future because it will only happen if it is God's will. It can be either endearing or completely infuriating because it is often misconstrued to allow complete inaction on the grounds that "**if it was meant to be done, God would make it happen**". With experience and once you get to know your colleagues better, you may be able to interpret the true meaning by the tone of voice adopted. Or you may not.

The teachings of the Prophet Mohammed are clear on this point and they urge people not to behave like a man without work sitting at home awaiting God to give him a job. Rather, the teachings urge people to go out and look for work and God will assist. It is rather more like the English saying of '**God helps those who help themselves.**' It can, however, be used for everything from an excuse for being late to a reason why no planning was done in preparation for an event. One of the most troubling for me is when I arrange to meet to discuss an important issue with a colleague and they simply retort as though it is completely out of their hands whether they are planning to turn up or not. But, of course, their religion requires them to say this.

There was a famous Arab intellectual and thinker in the middle of the last (20th) century called Abdulrazzaq Al Bossa who told the story of his own father. In 1932, when smallpox was in danger of taking a grip in the country, his father was taking his son to be vaccinated when he passed by the house of a neighbour. The neighbour asked where he was going and, on being told, remarked that, if it was God's will that his son would get smallpox, vaccination was therefore pointless and also an insult to God. Al Bossa's father was taken by this and, instead of taking his son for vaccination, he sat and drank coffee with his neighbour. Tragically, his son caught smallpox some few weeks later and from an early age lost his sight completely and never regained it. For the remainder of his days, his father bitterly regretted his decision and he ensured that his son grew up to understand the importance of doing everything in his power to help himself and not simply deferring to God's will.

Its modern misinterpretation can be worrying also. Why, indeed, do so few Gulf Arab mothers travel with their children in seat belts or young men racing their motorbikes wear crash helmets? Because their fate is in God's hands and, if it is God's will, what good will seat belts or helmets be? Is this what was truly meant by **Insh'allah** or is this a dangerous misinterpretation?

You may well disagree with the concept of fate as I have described it, but beware of any attempt to stop its use or even comment on it in a less than favourable manner.

I spent several months in Iraq during the coalition operation there in the early 2000s, advising the Governor and senior security officials in two Iraq provinces that were transitioning back to their own control from that of the Coalition forces. I had formed a close bond with a dynamic and influential senior Iraqi Army General and, when my tour ended, he invited me to a celebratory lunch. After a delicious meal, we moved to his office for sweets and coffee, and he asked me what single point they should improve over the next few months. Feeling relaxed and happy, and full of camel meat and dates, I told him and his officers that, in my opinion, the term Insh'allah was extremely unhelpful because it completely stopped any form of contingency planning from taking place and, therefore, we were constantly planning at speed and under pressure when things went awry, which they often did at the time.

I should have guessed that this was an ill-advised comment when my translator, a well-trusted and extremely well-educated Iraqi, stopped and asked if I really wanted to say this to the General. I replied that of course I did, and he duly translated. The temperature in the room appeared to drop several degrees and my farewell lunch ended abruptly because my advice had been taken as an insult against Islam. I had received another good lesson in understanding the DNA, the grain, and working with it and not across it. I never made that mistake again.

How to counter this issue? Endless amounts of patience and, if you do decide to tackle the issue head-on, steer well away from making any comment that may be interpreted as criticism of Islam. And the very best of luck to you.

Face. The maintenance of face is another key characteristic of any Gulf Arab person, and they will go to great lengths to avoid its loss. Indeed, it is probably the most important single Arab trait because from this comes the original Bedouin Arabs' characteristics of loyalty, bravery, manliness and hospitality. Gulf Arab people strive to ensure that everything will be done to avoid any sign of weakness being displayed, that the Arab does not present themself in a poor light and certainly that they do not allow themself to be portrayed in a poor light. This can result at worst in the avoidance of difficult decisions or situations and a reluctance to share bad news with you, and at best in your leaving a discussion believing that you have an agreement only to find later that this is not the case because the Arab did not want you to lose face by a firm rejection – because it works both ways.

Raphael Patai sums this up in his book: 'A simple Assent can be for him nothing more than a polite form of evasion while the same word may mean to an English interlocutor a definite positive commitment.'

In our dealings with Gulf Arab people, we must also be careful to avoid being seen to push them into corners with a potential loss of face for the individual because this will result in a significant loss of respect for you as a manager or leader.

In the West, we see strength in leaders who are able to grasp the nettle. This is seldom the case with Gulf Arab people, and they may go to considerable lengths to avoid any form of direct confrontation. In Western eyes, this may be considered to be a lack of integrity, which is also a key Islamic and Arabic trait but, in the eye of the Arab, maintenance of their dignity trumps even this.

As one of the large companies that I worked for headed towards serious trouble through the family dispute that I described earlier, the senior leadership shut themselves away more and more as they appeared less able to find a solution and, rather than appear often among the workforce to add encouragement at a difficult time, they so feared the loss of face that they hid. This in turn only served to convince the workforce that we were in a terminal decline. Unfortunately, no long-term solution was ever found, and the Owners remained locked away dealing more and more through a small band of trusted individuals. More and more, the Owners blamed the failings on the expatriate senior managers who had been brought in to run the business, thereby allowing them to maintain face among their own community.

This trait is one of the most complex for us to understand and can manifest itself in so many ways. I am not certain that we can ever fully comprehend it. Accept it, however, because it is so fundamental to our ability to create a relationship that it must be understood and worked with. I have seen so many occasions in both the Army and in the business world where a failure to understand and accommodate this issue has resulted in the alienation of Westerners from the Arabs, sometimes with terminal results for the Westerners.

Relationships with Expatriate Workers. In many parts of the Gulf, most of the senior, middle and junior management jobs, and indeed all the menial jobs, are done by expatriate workers. The term "expatriate" in the West conjures up images of heavily suntanned Westerners, living the good life without the hindrance of having to pay taxes. The truth in the Gulf is somewhat different because the term is used for all migrant workers of any race. So, although some might be living the high-life, many are not.

Many workers, particularly from the Asian subcontinent, live in poor conditions, rarely travel to their homes to see their families, and are paid less well than the local nationals. Despite this, many of them manage to send financial support to their families in their home countries and they are often supporting not only their children but also a large extended family. These countries receive considerable income from their expatriates working abroad in what economists refer to as "Remittance Economics".

In some of the more progressive businesses, however, you will find expatriates in the most influential positions where they are completely trusted and have become a part of the "family".

Unfortunately, in the eyes of many Arabs, though, there is a racial bias against all expatriates and it can be a real management challenge to overcome this issue. In the most extreme cases, the expatriate is treated as a third-class citizen and it can be extremely difficult to experience. Paradoxically, the loyalty of many of these expatriate workers is unquestioning and strong towards any business, and they often stay for many years. For many, however, this is simply because the alternative is to return to their own country where there is either no work or at least no work with the same pay. The loyalty, therefore, is linked to their security of employment and a regular wage, which allows them to keep their families fed and housed back home. When a better offer appears, loyalty can and will be quickly switched.

This racial prejudice is not limited to the Arabs alone. In every business in the Gulf, there is a stratum of management and workforce with each level of the strata found from a separate nation. Each level of the strata believes that it is better than the level below and problems can arise when people feel that they are being asked to do a job that should be done by someone from a lower stratum.

I have faced several times the comment that what I have asked someone to do is not acceptable because they are not expected to do that sort of work as it is beneath them. The fact that I may be standing in front of them with my sleeves rolled up doing this particular job is further bemusing to them because as a Westerner and a senior manager, I certainly should not be doing this work.

My advice is to have absolutely no patience with this sort

of comment, continue leading from the front and sharing the most menial jobs, and eventually the workforce will stop considering you completely mad and may begin to understand the old maxim of **Serve to Lead**.

Despite the obvious challenges, managing or leading a multicultural team can be both challenging and enormously satisfying. You will have people in the team from a wide variety of ethnic, religious and social backgrounds, and if you can harness their potential and encourage them to give you their views you will have a hugely varied range of opinions to select from when you are required to make a decision. If you can encourage them to voice their honest opinions, you may well have workers or subordinates who can challenge your thinking in a positively disruptive way. This will not, however, happen overnight. What can be better than to come to not only a **Rice Solution** but also a **Fusion Solution!**

Time Management. I could not end this part of the book if I did not mention the Gulf Arab person's use of time:

> [The] **Gulf Arab** [person] **sees time as a precious resource which he must make the most of and he does not see any boundary between work and play. If something is worth doing then he will spend his time doing it and he will not waste time.** (Oxford Strategic Consulting: *The Gulf Arab Leadership Style*)

The pamphlet on management and leadership in the region from which the above quote is taken highlights the issue that the Western consideration of time and its influence on our behaviour is very different from the Arab mindset. Neither is necessarily more correct than the other, but they are different views of the same important subject. The outcome of the Gulf Arab people's approach can lead to conflict if it is not well understood.

The merging of the boundary between work and play allows the Gulf Arab person to see nothing unusual about completing a family meal in the evening and enjoying family time, and then returning to his business work from home. They will often make telephone calls late in the evening and do not be surprised if you receive important calls very late from a business colleague who will expect you to engage fully. This is particularly prevalent during Ramadan when the normal working routines are disrupted and the Arab will sleep late and work extremely late.

You must be prepared for this and receptive to it. It may be advisable to amend your own work patterns during Ramadan to accommodate it. Take it as a compliment if you receive a late call because it shows an acceptance from your Arab host.

I suspect that you, as a leader, want things to be run on time and, if you ask for a meeting at 10 a.m., you live with the expectation that at 10 a.m. people will have arrived, properly prepared for whatever is to follow and that, if there is another call on their time, such as a mobile telephone call, this will be dealt with by a simple refusal.

In reality, you can expect meetings to be constantly delayed by either late attendance or lack of attendance. Throughout the meeting, telephone calls will be taken. Be prepared for people to simply leave. Initial attempts to demand a stricter regime can be met with bemusement and laughter, as though a stricter adherence to timing is a rather curious Western invention.

As a slightly ironic aside, it never ceases to amaze me, however, that some of the earliest time-keeping devices were actually found in Egypt dating back from some 1500

BC. It is curious that so many years ago the people from this part of the world were so intent on maintaining the correct time. What on earth has happened in between time?

This is one of those management issues that you will need to make a judgement on and work out in your own mind how you are going to accommodate the Arab view of time. Using the Arab culture to effect, I have had some success explaining that being late for me gives me the impression that the individual considers their time more important than mine because mine was simply being wasted in waiting. This is extremely disrespectful and, of course, I know that it is not the individual's intention to be disrespectful. I have often asked individual employees if they would ever be late if the Emir or the King asked them to visit. Of course, they say 'No'. Then it is simply that they do not hold me in the same position of respect.

An alternative strategy is to book every meeting with an in-built expectation that people will be at least 15 minutes late!

CHAPTER 6

Gulf Arab Company Structure and Management

Company Structure

It is extremely important that we understand the structure at play in any organization that we join or do business within the Gulf. Throughout the region, it is most likely that the workforce will be extremely multicultural in all companies from the largest multinational to the smallest family-owned business. Within an organization, there will be strata of management and workers with each level often being found from a particular nation as previously discussed in Chapter 5. You should quickly identify the makeup of the various levels and be prepared potentially to adapt your style of leadership and management to gain the most from each.

The way you chose to lead or manage your junior management team, who may be Asian, may be subtly different from the way you lead or manage the Egyptian shop floor workers, for example, and the adage of one size fits all may not be appropriate. As an example of this, I would suggest that allowing or encouraging the use of freedom of action and initiative from every member of your team from the start may simply result in utter confusion. They may not be as used to it as you are and may even see this freedom as proof that you are not certain, yourself, what to do.

Main Board. The main Board of any business is likely to be from leading families from whichever country you find yourself in. In family companies, the business may have been established by one or two former family members who will have worked extremely hard to graft out a prosperous business from the desert. Sons, cousins and sometimes daughters and nieces will have inherited their place on the Board, some more deserving than others – more of this later on.

Gulf Arab people have a saying that any family business will only last three generations: the first generation establishes the business; the second lives off the profits; and the third destroys it. This is not limited to Gulf Arab businesses because there is a saying in the North of England that in any family business 'You will go from clogs to clogs in three generations.'

There will be some Board members who style themselves as Directors and have a very hands-on approach to the business, in which case their leadership style will be vitally important and influential. Others will be content to leave the daily workings of the business to the CEO and the senior management team, and to take very little part in the daily running of the company. Every Board will be different, however, and, as you complete your due diligence before accepting the job or planning a business agreement, try and identify as much as you can about the relationship of the Board to the senior management team and, in particular, try and gauge the strength of the relationship between a) the CEO and the Board, and b) the Board and the senior management team.

Here are a few things to look for:

Main Board Composition: As previously discussed, most Board members in family companies will have inherited their position through family links and many will be completely professional and see it as their family duty to run the business as well as they can. Some members, however, will be either unwilling or simply unable to provide relevance to the business because they represent part of the family and do not have a particular skill or range of experience. In the worst cases, they will be involved simply to ensure that they receive their financial dividend from the business. This type of contribution was once described fittingly by a Gulf Arab friend of mine as **Greed Leadership.** Because of the family nature of the business, there may be a reluctance to identify where the Board's weaknesses lie, and then to try and address them through bringing on to the Board people to provide the missing skills and experience.

Few Board members will have completed a thorough apprenticeship in the business and, therefore, their detailed knowledge may be very lacking. The young family members who are likely to inherit the business may well have a list of business qualifications gained from the best management schools and universities in the West. However, many will have been reluctant to taste life as a junior or middle manager to see how their business really works. Only a few will have spent time on the shop floor because many would consider that to be demeaning to their position within the company. Without this detailed knowledge, however, they would find it very difficult to control the business as one would expect from a Main Board. Many of the greatest corporate failures throughout history have occurred because the Board has failed to understand its business sufficiently well and has focused on irrelevant or inaccurate information that is not critical to business performance.

In many of the major companies throughout the Gulf that have been heavily influenced by Western methods, some of the attitudes found within family companies are, of course, much less apparent. The leadership will be highly trained and motivated, and will follow closely Western, often American, business practices.

CEO: Look at the key relationship between the Board and the CEO. It is vitally important that this works well and, in particular, that the CEO has the ability to speak honestly and robustly when required. They must be able to challenge the Board without the Board seeing this as somehow unwarranted, or worse – threatening to their own status or face. Similarly, the Board must have the ability to challenge the CEO.

Boards that comprise several founder families can be particularly vulnerable to the playing of power politics, which can be incredibly destructive for the business. If there is no coherent vision from the Board as to the direction of the business, then there will be problems. Alternatively, the Board may avoid all difficult conversations among themselves so as to ensure that harmony is maintained throughout the Board. This, also, will not work for long.

I have to admit that I took one job without having done sufficient investigation and due diligence on the management, and I immediately found myself in the midst of a bitter dispute between Owners. Without any warning and certainly no preparation, I found myself one of several pawns in a damaging battle between the Directors and the CEO.

Management: Under the Board will be a level of senior management that, dependent on the company, will come from Western countries and will be motivated and professional in the main, although a minority will be driven by money alone and all the benefits of tax-free living in the sun. Identify them quickly and again adapt an appropriate management style (or simply avoid them). On rare occasions, the worst of these mostly Western expatriates will be in positions that they would not expect to fill in their own countries, and their poor performance is exacerbated by an unwillingness or a failure to grasp the cultural nuances of their appointment.

So much of the effectiveness of the senior management will be decided upon by the relationship between them and the Board.

Under this group will come a level of junior management found mostly from the Asian sub-continent or the Levant. These are likely to be well educated and extremely loyal to the business, but they can be strict followers of policy and regulations and may not have been brought up in an environment of empowered initiative. They will require close supervision with clear guidelines.

Workforce: Below the middle and lower management will come a workforce either from those other Arab countries without oil wealth or from the Asian sub-continent. They will be loyal and in the main hardworking, but they are not likely to be paid very well.

Right at the bottom of the strata will be a group of highly loyal people doing menial jobs. Examples are junior office workers who, again, are likely to be from the Asian sub-continent. They will generally be poorly paid but incredibly loyal and willing.

Remember, however, that loyalty can be bought.

Increasingly throughout the Gulf countries, Arabization is taking place at a pace and there is, therefore, a consequent reduction in reliance on expatriate workers. Incentives from their Governments often exist to employ Arabs and many can be financially rewarding for the business. It is important, however, to understand and work with some of the cultural issues that may be present in your Arab workforce. There are, of course, many exceptions to the rule but timekeeping, work ethic, family loyalties and racial prejudice against other nationalities may all be present and must be handled with care.

Females in an Organization: One of the great

misconceptions in the Gulf is that females are subservient in every way in society including business. This is simply wrong. In several countries in the region, female leaders have been present in business for years. Recent lifting of restrictions in countries such as Saudi Arabia has opened the door to well-educated and highly motivated females who certainly have something to prove. The female "genie is out of the bottle" and it is exciting to see more and more businesses with highly motivated and ambitious females at every level. Some young males who have allowed themselves to develop a sense of entitlement may increasingly find themselves losing out to women in the workplace.

The presence of women in the workplace can have an extremely positive effect on the work ethos of young Arab men. They often look to the women and very quickly see that they may have to come to work a little earlier or simply smarten themselves up. A good friend of mine who is CEO of a leading Saudi company in oil and gas told me to look at the shoes of the young Arab men once young women started in the business because, very quickly, they will start to look more business-like in their appearance.

CHAPTER 7

Gulf Arab Leadership and Management Culture

Having now looked at some of the context, both Islamic and Arabic, for the workplace, I would like to turn our attention to how in reality these traits manifest themselves into what might be termed "a Gulf Arab leadership and management style". Of course, this style will not be the same everywhere and there will inevitably be many Arabs in the workforce or in positions of leadership who have been educated and heavily influenced by business schools and universities abroad, particularly in the West. There are, however, several strong traits that will be present to a greater or lesser extent in any business.

Relationship-Oriented: Relationships are key to success when working for the Arabs. Many books have been written on the subject and, in particular, the need to take time to develop strong and enduring relationships that may take months to achieve and, by the way, a huge consumption of strong coffee, sweet tea and dates. This approach is completely alien to many Western businesses that are understandably driven by profit and loss margins and seeking to exploit every meeting to their own advantage. Such an approach, though, where time is not given for pleasantries and ice breaking, can be considered not just rude but also completely self-defeating by the Arabs.

Over several years, I have witnessed so many companies that have sent their senior management to the Gulf to secure business and who have acted as follows:

- They have demanded meetings on a Friday (the Islamic holy day), because it suits their own programme (as they have travelled extensively bagging opportunities on the way and they want to be back by the weekend!);

- They have assumed a close relationship that they have not taken the time to create (and some have even immediately attempted to kiss their hosts on their first meeting, which is both awkward and thoroughly embarrassing);

- they have tried to avoid all the pleasantries and small talk by "cutting" straight to the point; and
- they have left with a smug view that the Arab has been extremely impressed by the fact that this high-powered member of the management team has taken time out to come personally.

In reality, the Arab is left feeling patronized at best and insulted at worst. In both cases, the effect will be the same: no relationship and, therefore, ultimately, no business.

In exactly the same way within a company, time taken to develop relationships with the managers and workforce is vitally important and will pay dividends in the future. The Arab will work well and do business with those people they like and, as we have discussed previously, if you have not taken the time to develop a relationship, they have enough cultural characteristics to avoid doing anything at all, should they decide to impede you. Be prepared to enter a meeting with your list of important points, but be satisfied if at the end you have achieved one or two only – that is, after all, progress. Certainly, to begin with, try and be satisfied with small steps (*Khotwat Sagheera* in Arabic) and gradually build to larger ones.

In the business environment, harmony is extremely important and time will be spent during the day to develop these relationships. What we may consider a complete waste of time, the Arab will consider a necessary part of developing a strong and productive relationship. Remember that the process cannot be rushed and nor are you controlling the pace. In the West, we can be reluctant to mix our working and social lives, but it is important that you are happy to talk about your family with the Arab to allow them to get to know you. You might also consider doing some homework on the subject of football because everyone will want to know what team you support and how they are doing in the league: it is a universal language and can be a great "ice breaker".

Management through a Group of Favoured People: As also discussed previously, it is important to identify the management strata in any business. This is not always immediately apparent and will take time. The Owners or Directors of any business are likely to work through a very small group of favoured people who will be in the senior management roles and whom they will have come to respect and see almost as members of their extended family. This paternalistic style of leadership can be extremely effective for those in the inner circle. But it can lead to some managers and workers feeling excluded.

However, it can also lead the favoured manager to lose a level of critical objectivity with the Owners or Directors as the individual places their favoured position above all else. This must be guarded against because every business requires a level of self-criticism among the top levels of leadership.

What is much less straightforward is to understand who are, what I would term the **power brokers** and probably even the **spies** in an organization. Both are likely to be present and both are in a position to wield extraordinary influence and power. It is really important that you take the time to work out this environment before you rush to make decisions.

The power brokers are those people within the organization who have a strong loyalty to the Owners or

Board members through family, tribe, long-term friendship or simply financial gain. They will have direct access to one or all of the Board members and they will exercise this on a regular basis despite, in some cases, not being in the higher management of the business. They will be prepared to bypass the organizational management chain within the company if they disagree with a decision that you have made, and this behaviour is often encouraged by the members of the Board. They may also be used by the Board members to influence decisions or to pass comment.

You need to first) work out who these people are and who their mentor is, then) understand how these people operate, and above all) handle them with great care. If they take against you for some reason, they can be extremely quick to try and damage your reputation at any opportunity with the Owners or Directors. They can, however, also be extremely useful to you as a sounding board for initiatives – "How do you think Mr X will react to this if I was to suggest it?" – or just for passing information to the Board. In any case, my advice is to handle them with extreme care!

The power brokers are most likely to be native Arab speakers and I remember the old maxim that a senior Kuwaiti General told me: 'Meetings may be done in English, but deals will be done in Arabic.'

Spies are present in every organization and it is sensible to assume that someone is telling the senior leadership or Board members exactly what is going on in any department. The spy may be a junior office worker or another employee, but they will be gaining financially from the deal and looking to gain favour with whoever their boss is. It is very difficult to stop this and you may have to simply accept that this is the grain.

Directive Leadership Style: Under Board level, the most frequent style of leadership displayed by Arab managers may be authoritarian or autocratic. Little scope is given to discussion or feedback and instructions are given with the simple expectation that they will be delivered to the letter. The style links to much of the Arabic culture that we have discussed earlier and, in particular, the belief in the superior position of the Arab within the business and the old maxim of leading and service. Their approach will be linked closely with the vision of the Board of Directors and is often characterized by very close supervision of individuals, which many may consider to be excessive over-management.

This can be extremely effective, however, particularly within a multicultural organization where freedom of action and use of initiative are not so prevalent in the national culture. Close supervision of clearly stated directives is a sensible way forward and can be extremely effective.

For those of us brought up in organizations that thrive on initiative at every level and who would prefer a more democratic style of leadership, the authoritarian approach can be a little difficult to stomach. But beware, as a manager or leader trying to move too quickly to introduce either your own democratic style or even a completely laissez-faire style, because it may be misinterpreted as a weakness, as my experience proved. It is worth bearing in mind that democratic leadership works best where there is a skilled and highly motivated workforce that are keen to share knowledge and best practice with each other. A culture where good ideas are jealously protected by an individual may not be the best environment for this form of leadership.

There are several research bodies that have carried out

studies into the effects of how values in the workplace are influenced by culture. One among these is the Hofstede Centre, under the leadership of Professor Geert Hofstede, which has carried out extensive research into this subject. The researchers apply several criteria to characterize a national character and then test an individual's leadership or management approach against them to give an indication of how effective their style is likely to be.

I paid a small remittance and completed a questionnaire to gain a view as to how effective my leadership and management style was likely to be with the Kuwaitis.

I consider my style to be mostly democratic and even laissez faire, and at all times in my career I have sought to encourage and stimulate the use of initiative and freedom of action in order to encourage peoples' development and to gain the very best from them.

However, when my leadership and management style was tested against the Kuwaiti culture, the Hofstede Culture Compass, as it is known, had a very different view of my abilities and commented:

Your subordinates may get the feeling that you do not want to be on top of the business by delegating too much, apparently because you cannot cope with all the responsibility put on your shoulders.

It went on to say:

You may demotivate your subordinates if you are not giving sufficient guidance to them.

This is a great example of turning the telescope the other way around and seeing oneself with the eyes of the Arab, in this case the Kuwaitis. I now have two choices: 1) ignore the result and drive forward in the manner to which I have become accustomed (and indeed trained) and run the risk of losing the subordinates, or 2) amend my approach: go with the grain or go against it – Rice Solution or Potato?

Initiative: I was brought-up with, and have always tried to develop, a mindset of freedom of action and the maximum use of initiative in every workforce that I have been involved with. It is both empowering for the individuals and also allows you as the leader or manager to concentrate your time on the most important issues. I have to admit that I have struggled a little with this issue in the Gulf and now follow the maxim that **"that which is not supervised is simply not done"**.

In the Arab culture, giving an individual too much freedom of action can be seen as your not wanting to take full responsibility for that action and there is a danger that you may lose face if you delegate too much.

You should expect to see individual goals and targets given with very little room for discussion or a two-way flow of ideas before decisions are made and very little feedback either asked for or given. There are clearly dangers with this approach but it can be extremely effective if you are prepared to accept the lack of personal development for your workforce. The danger comes when the decision maker is away for a protracted period because little can happen without direct delegation.

CHAPTER 8

Cultural Behaviour in the Business Environment

Having discussed in previous chapters the leadership and management styles that you are likely to encounter, it is important to understand some simple protocols and practices that will allow you to gain the most from your work in the Gulf or your business trip.

As with everything, the time that you take in preparation will pay dividends. I have covered much of this earlier, but here are a few things to consider:

Meetings: Business meetings are the staple diet of business life in the Arab world as much as they are in the West. The main difference, however, is the expectation in the minds of the sponsor of the meeting as to what can be achieved. You should not change your approach to meetings, but you should alter your expectation as to how much you will achieve. Always attend any meeting with an agenda of points that you wish to discuss, but be prepared to cover only one or two and, initially, while you are in the stage of developing working relationships, be prepared to cover none of them. This is not wasted time but the reverse, because you are talking and working on a relationship that will bear fruit in the future.

If you are proposing a business meeting with a Gulf Arab person from outside the country, it is a very good idea to have an agent or representative in the country to set it up on your behalf. Of course, the meeting must not be proposed on a Friday or Saturday because that is the weekend, and a request for a meeting on either of those days will cause confusion at best and offence at worst.

Do not be surprised, despite a meeting having been set up several weeks before, that it is cancelled at short notice due to an alternative commitment that will probably be related to a family reason such as the requirement to attend a Condolence for someone who has died: these events will always take precedence. As an aside, the person who set up the meeting may also forget to tell you until you have arrived!

If you are planning to write a letter of introduction or to present your business card, it is very well worthwhile having them translated into Arabic. Be careful, however, where you have this translation done. Some translators are not good: they will simply use 'Google Translate' or other web-based translation tools and the results can be awful, funny or – at worst – insulting. When I first arrived in Kuwait my first attempt at translating a business card caused much hilarity with my hosts in the Kuwaiti Ministry of Defence because, instead of stating that I was with the British Armed Forces, it said that I was a member of a well-known Shia Militia; not at all helpful but thankfully seen and corrected before I had spread too many.

It is good practice to have everything that has been translated into Arabic translated back to you in English to provide a check that it is as you want it. I once wrote a report for a business recommending that a pilot course should be completed to properly test a proposal. This was translated as a course for pilots, which caused great confusion and a belief that I had completely missed the point. It can be extremely time-consuming completing this double translation, but it can be time very well spent.

Corresponding with business contacts can be a frustrating process. Emails often go unanswered, particularly if they have some negativity (such as following up on an unpaid invoice) and this can be extremely difficult. Many Arabs see other forms of social media, such as WhatsApp, to be their primary form of communication. You should identify the best way to correspond and use that. A simple method is to ask the person directly how they wish to communicate and then use that method. As you develop your business relationships, Arabs like regular contact and use of the voice message application on WhatsApp provides a simple way of sending messages in a more personal way, which is often appreciated. Rather than send a detailed email that may be misinterpreted or not even read, I often use this function in everyday correspondence.

If you are corresponding with an Arab to relay bad or unpalatable news, you should expect either no reply or at least a very delayed one.

Clothing: There is always a temptation to dress down in the Gulf because of the heat. Gulf Arab people, particularly the older generation, are by nature conservative and I would suggest that you wear a suit and tie or smart office wear for ladies to a first meeting and then gauge what alternative may be acceptable from that. I once took a very senior British Army Officer, who had taken the opportunity of travelling between Iraq and the UK to meet his opposite number in the Kuwait Armed Forces. Because he was travelling in the height of the summer, he was wearing a linen suit with no tie and suede desert boots. After the meeting, which had appeared to go extremely well, the senior Kuwaiti commented to me that it was clearly not a serious meeting because the Officer was wearing boots and no tie. Some years after this event, I was telling this story to a now recently retired senior British Army Officer who asked me if it was indeed he who had been the culprit. I could not tell a lie.

Greeting: As I have already said, a few words of greeting in Arabic will always be well received and there is no expectation that you will be able to continue in fluent

Arabic, although wonderful if you can. As you enter any meeting room, you may be surprised that there are many more people there than you were expecting. Some will have been specially invited to the meeting and some may just have been passing and wished to pay their respects. Do not be put off by the numbers, but simply introduce yourself to each person and shake hands with each one in turn. If it is a formal meeting, there may be orderlies or waiters ready to provide snacks or drinks and I strongly suggest that you do not include them in your handshaking since that may appear a little odd. If there are Arab women present and you are a man, my advice is that you introduce yourself by name but do not proffer a hand – allow the woman to take the lead. Some Arab women are very comfortable with this but others are not and, even if you put your hand out, they may simply ignore it, which will be embarrassing for you. Simply place your hands across your chest or one hand over your heart as a mark of respect.

Above all, try and avoid the temptation to attempt to kiss your hosts on first meeting and, in my opinion, this should be avoided completely until the Arab is ready to initiate the action. This may never occur and it is not a sign that they do not like or respect you, but simply that they understand that it is not in your culture and they do not wish to embarrass you or cause you to lose face in any way.

You will be asked to sit at the side of your host and nobody will be in a hurry to initiate the business discussion. Let them take the lead. You will be offered coffee and drinks, and you should accept. The small **Finjan** of strong Arabic coffee smelling strongly of cardamon should be accepted and the waiter may hover waiting for you to return the cup that he will then refill or offer to another guest. A small sidewards shake of the cup will signify that you do not want a refill and he will simply move on. If instead you pass the cup back to him without the shake, you will receive the cup back again refilled... and again... and again.

Try and avoid sitting with your legs crossed with your feet raised and, worst of all, pointing the soles of your shoes at your host. In the Arab culture, showing someone the bottom of your feet or your shoe soles is extremely rude. Many will remember the pictures at the end of the last Iraq war when the statue of Saddam Hussein was pulled over and the local Iraqis beat it with their shoes.

There may be occasions when your Arab host will hold your hand. This should be taken as a great compliment to you and a sign of developing trust. Do not withdraw your hand: accept the compliment with good grace.

Developing Relationships: Developing a relationship with someone whom you are planning to do business with is extremely important to the Gulf Arab person, as already discussed in Chapter 7. The first meeting may not get beyond pleasantries and some general discussion. My advice is that you must be patient and avoid having a long list of points that you wish to cover. You may find that your host will look nervous and they will certainly not understand the rush at all. Above all, they will not feel at all pressured to work at your pace and they may simply just consider you pushy at best or rude at worst.

Do not expect important decisions to be made at early meetings since the process of developing a relationship must be allowed to take place at the pace of the Arab and not you. Be patient and be prepared to be summoned for a return meeting at relatively short notice because a decision may have been made unexpectedly. I refer to this practice as the '**instantly melting glacier**' whereby progress can appear to be extremely slow, which will cause you to think that it has stalled completely. Then, suddenly and often without warning, a decision is made with an expectation that everything can be delivered instantly. This is particularly the case with large and complex projects that are working their way through a tender process. It is as well to always maintain the dialogue and try and gauge the progress or otherwise of any issue or project.

Look for opportunities yourself to develop the relationship and there will be certain local customs that will enable you to achieve this. In several countries in the Gulf, the men, and more commonly now women, will meet together on set evenings of the week in a **Majlis** or **Diwanyah**. Often, they will sit over food or coffee and there will often be a large television showing a football match. People will come and go throughout the evening and they will always welcome visitors. A visit to one of these provides a wonderful opportunity for you to sit and chat informally to develop relationships, meet new people and expand your network.

Find out the local custom and embrace it. It may require you to take a deep breath for the very first time before you enter a room full of strangers, but it is always worth it and your Arab host will be greatly complimented by your attendance. Throughout the Gulf, when a family member dies, the family will gather together to accept the Condolences of wider family members, friends and colleagues. This may sometimes take place at set hours over a period of several days. Attendance at a Condolence provides an opportunity to show deep respect to your Arab colleague or friend. There is no equivalent in Western culture to this and the nearest to it is possibly the wake. A wonderful old woman whom I never met was particularly kind to my wife when we first arrived in Kuwait. When she died, I attended the Condolences of the men of her family. I stayed for a very short time, but I was able to meet her son and thank him for the kindness his mother had shown to my wife. The family often commented on my visit for years afterwards because it had made a strong impression.

We have discussed the importance of face to Gulf Arab people and remember that this works both ways. Someone may not want to disappoint you at a meeting, thereby causing you to lose face, by, for example, their not conceding to one of your requests. They may well, therefore, leave you with a response that appears positive but is actually completely non-committal and certainly not a binding decision. I have been at so many meetings when the business visitor has come out confident that they have achieved a positive decision only to have their hopes dashed when they follow up at a later date.

This can all be a little frustrating but beware because the single easiest way to lose face and destroy a relationship is to show this – or, worse still, any signs of anger – publicly. You must remain calm and polite throughout, and avoid the temptation to share your real feelings because it may very simply have the completely opposite effect to the one you are hoping for.

Once you have taken the time to get to know the Gulf Arab people with whom you are about to do business, you will quickly learn that they are charming, immensely hospitable and will display a ready wit and a great interest in your opinion. Meetings become something to look forward to and you will start to reap the rewards of your patience, calmness and good humour.

Local Agents: In most countries in the Gulf, you will find it almost impossible to achieve a meeting or break into a business without an agent. An agent is a local national who is well connected in your line of business and therefore able to open doors for you. Finding a good agent can be very difficult and a sensible starting point is to contact the trade department of your own Embassy in the country. In turn the Embassy staff are likely to put you in touch with the local Business Forum. These exist in most of the countries in the region. A Business Forum is not only a source of extremely good advice but also a useful networking forum for work.

Arab Language: It can be said that there are three elements that define an Arab: Islam, the Gulf and, thirdly, the Arab language. The Arab language, like Islam, has strong roots in the past and has not developed as some other Western languages have – in particular, English. In 2018, *The Oxford English Dictionary* added 1,100 new words to its edition. In the same year, there were no known additions to the Arab vocabulary. Arabic in the business context is often considered to be extremely limited as a result. Educated Gulf Arab people have adopted a language that switches from Arabic to English apparently at will. It is interesting to note that many national radio stations in the Gulf such as Bahrain Radio and Saudi Aramco's Energy Radio broadcast completely in English. Could we be seeing the slow process of the Arabic language disappearing from the wealthy and middle classes?

Most business meetings will be held in English and there is seldom an expectation that you will understand Arabic. It is, however, the side discussion or **noises off**, that the theatre world describes, which can be so useful to have an understanding of. Arabic is not easy to learn but, if you can, certainly a few words of pleasantries will be very well received.

Humour: Dwight D. Eisenhower, the American soldier, politician and President commented that 'A sense of humour is part of the art of leadership, of getting along with people, of getting things done.'

As with every culture, verbal humour is a key element of developing relationships with Arabs. The sense of humour is different, however, and one must be attuned to this in your dealings. You only need to look at Arab TV stations, such as Nile TV, which you may have flicked past on your hotel TV, to watch the type of gentle and rather picaresque comedy that is loved throughout the Gulf to see the stark differences. In Western culture, gentle teasing or "mickey-taking" can be deployed without a great risk of causing offence. It can even serve to create a bond of friendship between individuals because it demonstrates a level of mutual warmth and even trust. It has a subliminal message that our relationship has reached a level where I am confident to tease you. This is not always the case with the Arab who may see it as an attempt to belittle him, particularly if the teasing is done in front of others. It is directly related to the face issue. Gentle teasing that in any way highlights weakness, or can be perceived as highlighting weakness, in an individual can be taken very badly. You can appear arrogant and attempting to be superior. Neither are enjoyed by your Arab hosts or business partners.

On a visit to my Saudi partner's workshop, I was greeted by one of his sons who was being employed as a manager at the workshop. I knew the son very well and liked him enormously. He was educated in both the USA and the UK and had a lovely sense of humour. We greeted each other very warmly with much laughter and hugging. At one point, I jokingly referred to him as the "spy" in the camp and we all laughed. The next day I was visited by the Saudi partner who told me that I had embarrassed his son in front of others and that my behaviour was completely unacceptable. He refused to accept my apologies and then raised a complaint with the Chairman of the Board in the UK. I explained to everyone that my comment had been extremely ill-judged and apologized to everyone concerned, particularly the son who was mortified by the whole experience. This was a simple example of a lighthearted remark that caused a loss of face for both the son and his father. Thankfully, not long afterwards, the incident was parked but maybe not completely forgotten.

One should also be wary of deploying clever turns of phrase, such as irony or puns, in comments because they are likely to be completely misinterpreted or misunderstood. At best, they will be completely ignored; at worst, they will be seen as an attempt to gain advantage. Sarcasm, too, should be avoided because, by its definition, it can be considered an aggressive remark that carries humour and, therefore, potentially offensive.

I have shared many humorous occasions with most Arabs, and I am not at all suggesting that you approach your business life in the Gulf with a lack of humour. Eisenhower was certainly right on this. I only suggest that you think a little deeper than you might at home before deploying the cutting and incisive wit that you alone may find extremely humorous.

CHAPTER 9

Old Ideas Out

Having looked at the individual leadership and management characteristics in the previous chapters, this chapter will look at some of the common challenges that may be faced when doing business in the region. Again, each country has its own particular characteristics, but there are several common themes that are common across all countries to a greater or lesser extent.

The business environment in the region is developing at a considerable pace with United Arab Emirates (UAE) and Qatar traditionally leading the way. In recent years, however, nowhere has the pace of change been greater than in the Kingdom of Saudi Arabia where the Crown Prince's ambition has been captured in the 2030 Vision.

The scale of the ambition is breathtaking, exemplified by some of the Giga and Mega projects that are in process, such as NEOM. However, there are some challenges remaining in the business environment as the Gulf develops its business and governance to deliver change at a rapid pace.

It was the British military theorist, Sir Basil Liddel Hart who commented:

> **There is only one thing more difficult than getting a new idea in, and that is getting the old idea out.**

He was referring to the military mind specifically, but this statement is very true in the business sector throughout the Gulf.

In many countries, the **"old idea"** can be defined as one where multilevels of bureaucracy existed, with each level passing responsibility upwards until finally the most senior individual could "sign off" any decision and where individual initiative was not encouraged. Low-level corruption was seen as the normal method of bypassing or speeding up decisions and was, therefore, widely accepted. Many of these countries, particularly those on the trade routes from the former British India, were heavily influenced by the British Indian Civil Service and indeed, up to relatively recently, the Indian Rupee was the currency. Many of the old ideas had their roots firmly in the bureaucratic methods so beloved of the Indian Civil Service.

The "**new idea**", however, is one where bureaucracy is minimized and automated with more and more completed online, managers are empowered to make decisions at the correct level and corruption in any of its many forms is eradicated.

The region is still transitioning from old to new and this can cause some very real business challenges. In the worst cases, the presence of old ideas can be best described as a **permafrost** through which vision and ambition are having to permeate typified by some "old and very conservative thinking". It can be confusing, time-consuming and extremely frustrating to navigate a path through it. This permafrost is thawing quicker in some countries than others, but it will be with us for a few years to come, I suspect.

On a recent contract with a major semi-government client, we were expecting an overdue purchase order to arrive to allow us to invoice for the work done correctly. When the document eventually arrived, extremely late, it had no less than eight approving signatures on the document. Each signature had probably taken up to a working week to achieve, thereby causing a two-month delay. This highlighted a level of bureaucracy that not only diminished the empowerment of subordinates but also encouraged managers not to take responsibility for their actions.

Slow or Delayed Payments: As anyone who has been involved in business will know, **cash is king,** and the most profitable small medium enterprise can struggle and ultimately go under unless the revenue arrives in the bank from their clients on time. Not having enough cash in the bank at the end of the month to pay salaries and suppliers is an extremely uncomfortable position to be in. Late payment is still common in the Gulf and there are few laws to regulate the practice. Late payment interest is not legal and collection costs, such as establishing costly bank credit, cannot be recovered from a debtor unless there is a particular agreement that has been included in the contract.

Common practices can take the form of endless queries on invoices, challenging small amounts and stopping the complete invoice, blaming the delay on other departments over which your client has little or no influence or combinations – or all of these. We recently had an example where we were asked to change the punctuation on an invoice before they would accept it. This amendment created a further delay of over 15 days.

Local legal action to retrieve payments is very slow and costly, and there is no guarantee of success. As a result of this situation, debtors will often try and negotiate discounts in exchange for prompt payments.

E-Invoicing, which at least allows a business to track the progress of invoices, is becoming a more standard practice and is encouraged throughout the Gulf, but it is sensible to consider adding payment delay fees to any contract and also demanding advance payments for work. Neither are foolproof and they also rely on the goodwill of any client.

One should take it as normal practice that from signature of a contract and mobilization or delivery of a product or service, you should expect to wait at least 90–120 days for the first payment. Make sure that you have either requested an advance payment where you can, or you have a sufficiently robust cash reserve to see you through the initial period.

There are some measures being considered by some Ministries of Finance in the Gulf but the regulations particularly assisting small businesses remain in the clients' favour. In my opinion, it is the singularly most damaging issue for foreign investment in the region.

Corruption: Low-level corruption used to be an everyday part of the working environment. With every commercial proposal, there was an expectation that an amount of money would have to be paid to someone along the line to "oil" the process. Most countries in the Gulf have set up strong measures to eradicate corruption in any form, such as the **Nazaha** system in Saudi Arabia, which has an anonymous helpline and regular messages to one's mobile encouraging you to whistle-blow on any incidents. In some organizations, old ideas still exist, however, and corruption has not been completely eradicated. It can present itself at times, which can be shocking and surprising given that companies and organizations have firm anti-corruption and bribery regulations.

In a recent bid discussion with a major semi-Government organization, we were asked to pay an amount of money to the Contracts Manager, and he would ensure that our competitors' proposals were not put forward. As a British company working alongside a Saudi partner, we naturally had zero tolerance of any forms of corruption, and I had ensured that our legal team had advised us on a clear and unambiguous anti-corruption and bribery policy that strictly followed the local Law.

We paused the process to seek advice from our local Saudi partner and to ensure that we had a plan to win the project but in a legal and transparent way. My fear was that we were being set up to fail by the client and that he was testing to see if we were indeed straight.

After very careful consideration, we did several things. First, we started a log of all correspondence and actions with the company. Next, we sent an email in English and Arabic explaining that we thought there must have been a mistranslation and what was actually being requested, presumably, was a discount on our commercial proposal bid price. We did not immediately report the situation through the anti-corruption site because at that stage there was some ambiguity in the approach, and we did not wish to set a damaging "hare running" if it was a genuine misunderstanding. The response from the client would confirm our next steps.

Two things happened very quickly. First, a long series of WhatsApp messages between the company and my Business Development Manager were deleted. Second, we received a formal email thanking us for the offer and agreeing that a discount was exactly what was required. We subsequently produced a small discount on our initial offer price and resubmitted. At no point was this issue ever discussed again and we won the business. In subsequent meetings with the client, I always wanted to have the ability to see the "thought bubbles" above our heads as we discussed the new project!

In our dealings with the company involved, we have continued to be extremely cautious. We have ensured that every conversation relating to the contract has been by email or letter in English and Arabic, and that records are maintained of all meetings.

Stovepipes: In many businesses and government agencies throughout the Gulf, departments and branches are managed as very separate and independent stovepipes (or **'silos'**, as they are sometimes referred to). The flow of information between the stovepipes can be very poor and, in the most extreme examples, there is no communication at all between them and indeed people are discouraged from dealing with people in other departments. In Arabic, this is referred to as working like **snails inside their protected shells**. This can be extremely frustrating to work with and can easily lead to confusion and loss of time.

This characteristic may be related to the tribal loyalty issue that we discussed in Chapter 5 because the "tribe" is considered more important than the company.

On one occasion in Saudi Arabia, we had received a change order to a contract, but the Finance Department of the client company did not understand the change and refused to pay the increased invoice. I visited the client and sat with the Contracts Manager who made several amendments to the Change Order to clarify the situation and he signed it. I asked him what the next step was, and he informed me that the Change Order would be sent to the Finance Department. Keen to be paid several overdue invoices, I asked him how long that would take, and he replied that it would be several days because it had to be sent to the right person. When I asked him where the Finance Department was, he explained that it was up on the next level of the building but that he did not go up there. Frustrated, I asked for the amended Change Order, walked up the stairs and delivered the revised order to the

Finance Department who signed to say they had received the right order, which I duly walked back to the Contracts Manager. This time, we achieved success and our invoices were duly paid, but this is not always the case.

You should be alert to this in any business and be prepared to act as a bridge between departments or branches to try and ease business.

Bank Bureaucracy: Most, if not all, banks in the Gulf are regulated under Sharia law and practices, which in some cases are very different from those you will be accustomed to in your home country. Interest on credit is not legal and simple business overdrafts that can be flexible and allow a business to weather the storms of slow payment (as discussed earlier in this chapter) do not exist. The bureaucracy to achieve credit can be extraordinarily slow and complicated with credit risk committees requesting a mountain of documents and assurances. We have often had occasions where documents are out of date by the time they are seen by a bank's credit committee. This can be extremely frustrating because new documents have to be prepared. It is the same for locally owned businesses and our Saudi partner, who runs a wholly Saudi-owned business, faces the same delays as joint ventures or wholly-owned overseas companies. Understanding the situation that relates to your own business is vitally important, as is developing strong relationships with your relationship managers. Most critically, expect delay and ensure that you have a Plan B.

CHAPTER 10

If Things Go Wrong

For most people, the experience of working in the Gulf will be stimulating, fulfilling and great fun. Things can go wrong, however, and it is worth at least considering in advance what happens if the dream job in the Arabian Gulf turns out contrary to what you expected and becomes a potential nightmare.

Every expatriate has at least one story of a friend who had a difficult experience in the region and, although most end favourably, some do not. My advice is do not stress about the possibility of it happening and, most particularly, do not turn down the opportunity of working in an exciting environment for fear of things going wrong. Do a few simple things, however, to prepare yourself for an unexpected turn of events.

In this part of the guide, I will describe an experience that I encountered, and try and give some pointers as to how you might prepare yourself for such an eventuality.

I talked earlier about the first job that I took after leaving the Army. The business had been started in the 1950s by two close friends who were great business pioneers and it had grown into a multi-million dollar business in the intervening years. Once the founding friends had died, however, a damaging succession dispute developed very quickly over who would take over the reins of the business. This dispute had played out in the background for several years but, because the business was developing and performing extremely well, it had little adverse effect on the company. I arrived in the company two weeks after an extremely damaging Court case, however, in which the judge had ruled that, because of some share registration irregularities, the business was to be considered in law a 50/50 partnership, despite the fact that one of the families had some 70% of the shareholding. From the day of the judgement, the minority shareholder partners arrived back in the business determined to stamp their authority on the company and to undermine that of the majority family.

The full effects of this were not slow in materializing, however, when I was informed by the CEO after only three weeks that a challenge had been made against my employment in the company and, from that point, the minority shareholding family refused to sign my salary or allowances or the rent on my house. Furthermore, they refused to accept any paper with my signature. The low point in the job came when one of the Owners and Board members sent an email to the entire workforce stating that I was not to be talked to, and warning that legal proceedings would be taken against anyone giving me official information. It was not my best day in that particular organization. Thankfully, a strong rebuttal arrived very shortly but, if I had not thought at that stage that things were serious, I certainly did then!

The situation ran on for several difficult months with my status in the company undermined by the dispute until a subsequent legal ruling removed the minority shareholders from any daily input into the management of the business. Almost as quickly as the problem had arisen, it was solved, but a great deal of long-term harm had been done to the company that was never fully mended. The situation rumbled on well after I had left until eventually the business failed.

What lessons can be drawn from this experience?

Research. There is a common saying that **'If it looks too good to be true, then it probably is.'** In my excitement at being offered an excellent first job outside the Army, which matched my financial expectations and kept us in the Gulf for a little longer, I was guilty of not completing detailed enough due diligence on the company. In one of the interviews for the position, there was a brief mention of the family dispute and an impending court case, but it was brushed over because nobody expected or indeed was prepared for the eventual outcome. A very good friend of mine who ran a number of companies in the Gulf even commented to me over dinner that the business had severe problems but, in my naivety, I even took this as slightly sour grapes and did not follow up on his comments. I did not think to probe the issue and that was a definite mistake that had serious repercussions.

It can be difficult to achieve but, in your research into a company, take time, try and ask people who may have dealings with it. If you are lucky enough to know locals, then ask them what they know and finally raise it as a direct question at the interview stage. At least you can then make the right decision based on your own research.

Faced with more information concerning the family dispute and the potential outcomes, I would probably have still taken the job, but at least I would have been better prepared for the position I found myself in and I may have done some preparation in terms of confirming my exact position in law and ensuring that I had a sensible fallback plan.

Labour Law: Despite having a valid contract with the business, the Owners on one side were able to try and remove me from the business by making my life so difficult that I would leave. How wrong they were. Some Gulf Arab countries have a reputation for not treating the expatriate workforce well, but actually the Labour Laws are generally very supportive of the worker and there will be reasonably simple processes to go through to make a legal challenge. There are normally very user-friendly guides available on the websites of the countries' Ministries of Social Affairs and Labour, written in simple English and with advice for those involved in contraventions. Some Ministries also publish guides for expatriate employees and it is well worth reading these before agreeing to work in any country, and certainly before signing any form of contract. You may find some interesting points in the guides that may not have been covered in the interviews – for example, in some countries' Labour Laws, an expatriate cannot take leave for nine months after starting employment.

In your negotiation for any job, try and negotiate as good a package, as you can, for redundancy or failure to complete the probation period successfully. These measures are known as "Golden Parachutes" and they will serve to protect you financially if the job does not come up to initial expectations or turns sour. These can give you up to six months' payout, which will compensate you.

Once you have received a contract, always have it reviewed by a lawyer who is an expert in the country's Labour Laws. The Consular section of your own Embassy will have lists of recommended lawyers who, for a fee, will complete this service. This will give you the peace of mind that, if there is a dispute, your contract is legally binding.

Legal Challenge: Hopefully you will never have to make a legal challenge against your Gulf Arab employer but, if you do, you will require not only a lawyer who understands the Labour Laws but also a local lawyer to work on your behalf as you develop the case to be heard initially by a Ministry of Social Affairs and Labour (or its equivalent) investigative official.

Attendance at either the Ministry or, in the worst case, a Labour Court can be an extraordinarily challenging experience and you will require a local to know the right desk to go to, the right papers to complete and to help you understand the process that you are likely to go through. I was required to lodge a complaint against my employer that resulted in a court case that, thankfully, I was not required to attend. My first visit to the Ministry to set the ball in motion would simply have been impossible without the assistance of a local lawyer who was able to navigate his way through the mass of complaining humanity to the correct office and with almost all our papers correct. There will always be something missing: that is almost axiomatic. My basic grasp of Arabic was simply not good enough to understand the legal jargon, and directions from our very helpful Ministry investigation officer who gave me no great confidence when having read through my case notes said: 'I don't understand why you are not being paid.'

I was thankfully able to refrain from any clever and witty response, and my case moved swiftly to the next legal stage.

Patience: As long as you have the law on your side and even the backing of your company, be confident that you will win eventually. It may take more time than you would wish for, but it will work. My advice is to maintain your calm and continue to show loyalty and determination to the company if you are able, as I was, to remain with it. If your dispute is with the company, then trust in the legal system.

I gave the minority shareholding owner who had taken against me a large piece of my mind on many occasions. Luckily for me, however, I did it only on the running machine at the local gym and only in my head. It was extremely important that I remained utterly professional and trusted in the work that was being carried out on my behalf by the CEO and majority shareholders. Fits of pique or rage may not be considered helpful by anyone and may lose you the respect of people who have been supportive up to that stage.

Sponsorship: In most countries in the Gulf, employment contracts, work visas and sponsorship of individuals are all linked. Cancellation of a contract can result in your losing your work visa and, therefore, your right of abode in the country. Make certain that you are clear about the terms of early dismissal, termination of your contract and how many days' grace you will have to find alternative employment – or worse, leave the country.

A very senior executive of a large multinational retailing chain was recently called to the office of his CEO, sacked for a misdemeanour and, because this also resulted in the cancellation of his sponsorship by the company, he lost his work visa as well and had to leave the country in days. Thankfully, there were clauses in his contract that softened the blow financially and ensured that he was able to break his house rental contract. It can and does happen. Just make certain that it is not you and, if it is, you are as well prepared as you can be.

CHAPTER 11

Rice Solution

So, we have come to the point where I will attempt to draw some conclusions from what has been covered so far in this book.

Mental Approach: I talked in Chapter 1 about the mental approach that one should adopt to working in the Gulf and in Figure 10.1 I have tried to illustrate this in a simple diagram. A job in this region can be a wonderful opportunity and provides chances to work with people of many varied cultures, not just Muslim or Arab, and to learn from them different ways of tackling management issues.

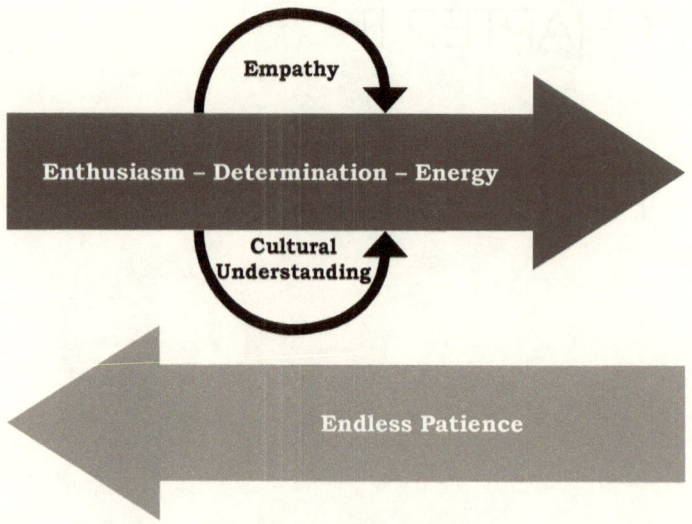

Figure 10.1 Attitude

Your mental approach must allow you to achieve what must appear to be an impossible challenge. You must maintain your enthusiasm, energy and determination to succeed while at the same time working to understand fully the people below and above you and the culture that you are immersed in. At the same time, you must be prepared to adopt a high degree of patience. The key here is to keep what appears to be conflicting requirements in balance. If one becomes the dominant factor, you may struggle to succeed. On occasions, you may have to be prepared to measure success in millimetres and not metres, but never lose sight of the eventual outcome or goal. This is all easier said than done, I know, and it requires you to constantly assess your own performance and that of your subordinates, but it can work.

I would like to leave you with one personal theory about how to assess the leadership and management culture of a country, and the beauty of this is that it can be done with relative ease on your way to the hotel when you arrive.

Roundabout Theory: The roundabout was first introduced in the USA as a traffic-calming measure in the early 1900s, but it was its adoption by the British in the 1960s as an important element of urban planning that made it extremely popular throughout the world. You will all understand the principle, I am certain: that the driver must give way to any traffic before entering the roundabout and must indicate before leaving to show their intention to leave. The driver requires a degree of understanding to make the measure a success, but mostly they require patience and a selfless commitment to road safety. In several countries throughout the world, however, the overriding requirement for drivers is sheer nerve to enter what is simply an irritating and completely pointless circle in the middle of a perfectly good road!

Driving safely on a roundabout requires an adherence to several principles that I have shown in Figure 10.2. These same principles are very similar to those of leadership and management.

Figure 10.2 Roundabout Driving Principle

Roundabout Theory

My theory is, therefore, that you can learn a great deal about the predominant culture from the method of tackling the roundabout. Those countries that adopt an aggressive and selfish approach to roundabouts will adopt the same approach to leadership and management, whereby personal gain and status are put above all else. To test my theory, I looked at the difference between the way the roundabout is driven in Kuwait to that of Dubai and the Emirates. My theory stood the test: different approach to roundabouts; different approach to business management and leadership.

I am of course making light of this important subject, but it may be worthwhile asking the taxi driver to travel via a roundabout at some stage before you start work or begin your first business meeting.

Moving to the Gulf should be an exciting adventure and the job may be your dream. You will be busy and challenged at work from the start. The region is full, however, of people who have moved out to a job but their families have not settled or enjoyed the experience and they have remained on their own as their families have relocated back to their home countries. This can be a lonely existence. Large multinational companies are likely to understand this fact better than small companies and will have relocation briefings and programmes aimed at the whole family. These can be extremely beneficial and allow you to make a family decision on any move to the Gulf. If you are going to join a small company, ask them for the same treatment and, at least, ask them to fund a family visit to the country to see the living conditions and, if required, the schools. Make this a family decision.

My final word is to offer you the best of luck and a sincere wish that you enjoy every minute of working in this exciting, challenging and wonderful Gulf region.

Bibliography

The Holy Qur'an

Adair, John. *The Action Centred Leader*. London, UK: The Industrial Society, 1988

Adair, John. *How to Grow Leaders. The seven key principles of effective leadership development*. London, UK: Kogan Page, 2009

Adair, John. *The Leadership of the Prophet Muhammad*. London, UK: Kogan Page, 2010

Al Khandari, Osama. *Eight Questions of Leadership - A study of Kuwait business*.

Barr, James. *A Line in the Sand - Britain, France and the Struggle that Shaped The Middle East*. London, UK: Simon and Schuster, 2011

Barr, James. *Lords of the Desert - Britain's Struggle with America to Dominate the Middle East*. London, UK: Simon and Schuster, 2018

Bowen, Jeremy. *The Making of the Modern Middle East*. London, UK: Picador, 2022

Clark, Michael (Professor). *Islam for Dummies*. London, UK: John Wiley & Sons, 2003

Davidson, Christopher M. *After the Sheikhs - The Coming Collapse of the Gulf Monarchies*. London, UK: C Hurst and Co (Publishers) Ltd, 2012

Fisk, Robert. *The Great War for Civilisation - The Conquest of the Middle East*. London, UK: Harper Collins Publishers, 2005

Ghattas, Kim. *Black Wave – Saudi Arabia, Iran and the Rivalry that Unravelled the Middle East*. London, UK: Headline Publishing, 2021

Hazleton, Lesley. *After the Prophet - The Epic Story of the Shia-Sunni split*. New York, NY: Doubleday, 2009

Hazleton, Lesley. *The First Muslim - The Story of Muhammad*. London, UK: Atlantic Books. 2013

Holland, Tom. *In the Shadow of the Sword - The Battle for Global Empire*. London, UK: Little, Brown & Co, 2012

Hussain, Ed. *The House of Islam*. London, UK: Bloomsbury Publishing, 2018

Jurd, Neil. *The Leadership Book*. London, UK: Mr Gresty, 2020

Lacey, Robert. *Inside the Kingdom*. London, UK: Arrow Books/ Penguin Random House, 2010

Lawrence, TE. *The 27 Articles*. London, UK: Simon and Schuster, 2017 (100th Anniversary edition)

Lawrence, TE. *Seven Pillars of Wisdom*. Oxford, UK: Oxford University Press, first published 1929

Lewis, Bernard. *The Arabs in History*. Oxford, UK: Oxford University Press, 1958

Maalouf, Amin. *The Crusades through Arab Eyes*. London, UK: Saqi Books, 2006

Patai, Raphael. *The Arab Mind*. New York, NY: Scribner, 1973 (later editions 1983, 2007)

Rogan, Eugene. *The Fall of the Ottomans - The Great War in the Middle East*. London, UK: Penguin Random House, 2015

Serve to Lead – The British Army's Anthology on Leadership. London, UK: The Royal Military Academy Sandhurst.

Sharp, Langley. *The Habit of Excellence - Why British Army Leadership Works*. London, UK: Penguin Books, 2022

Von Tunzelman, Alex. *Blood and Sand*. London, UK: Simon and Schuster, 2016

Williams, Jeremy. *Don't they know its Friday - Cross Cultural Considerations for Business and Life in the Gulf*. Dubai, UAE: Motivate Publishing, 1998

Further Reading

Recommended Reading List

After the Prophet: The Epic Story of the Sunni/Shia split in Islam by Lesley Hazleton. Doubleday, 2009. (ISBN 978-0-385-523-943)

A Line in the Sand: Britain, France, and the Struggle that Shaped the Middle East by James Barr. Simon and Schuster, 2012. (ISBN 978-1-847-394-576)

Black Wave – Saudi Arabia, Iran and the Rivalry that Unravelled the Middle East by Kim Ghattas. Headline Publishing Group, 2020 (ISBN 978-1-472-271-099)

Crusades through Arab Eyes by Amin Maalouf. Saqi Books, 2006 (ISBN 978-0-863-560-231)

Don't They Know It's Friday: Cross Cultural Considerations for Business and Life in the Gulf by Jeremy Williams OBE. Motivate Publishing, 1999. (ISBN 978-1-860-630-743)

Islam for Dummies, by Professor Malcolm Clark. John Wiley & Sons, 2003. (ISBN 978-0-764-555-039)

Letters to a Young Muslim by Omar Saif Ghobash. Picador, 2017. (ISBN 978-1-509-842-599)

Soldier in the Sand: A personal history of the modern Middle East by Simon Mayall. Pen and Sword Military, 2020. (ISBN 978-1-526-777-737)

The Arab Mind by Raphael Patai. WW Norton & Co, 2002. (ISBN 978-1-578-261-178)

The First Muslim: The Story of Muhammed by Lesley Hazleton. Atlantic Books, Penguin, 2013. (ISBN 978-1-594-487-286)

The Leadership of Muhammed by John Adair. Kogan Page, 2010. (ISBN 978-0-749-460-761)

The Twenty-Seven Articles by TE Lawrence. Simon & Schuster, 2017. (ISBN 978-1-501-182-006)

Newspapers

Arab News (Saudi Arabia) – www.arabnews.com

Gulf News (Bahrain) – www.gulfnews.com

The Khaleej Times (Dubai) – www.khaleejtimes.com

Author Biography

Edward Brown, MBE, has spent over 20 years working and living in the Arabian Gulf Region. Serving with the British Army for 37 years he deployed on operations in Iraq and Kuwait and towards the end of his service he was seconded on Loan Service to the Kuwait Armed Forces as the Brigadier, Commander of the British Military Mission, a role he fulfilled for 3 years. He left the Army to join a Kuwaiti family business which at the time had the Mercedes Benz franchise and spent 3 years running their operations department. He subsequently moved to be CEO of a Private Emergency Fire and Rescue Company in the Kingdom of Saudi Arabia (KSA), living between KSA and Bahrain. He remains in the position today. Developing his interest in Gulf Arab culture, early in 2015, and in his spare time, Edward established Rice Solutions Co delivering cultural awareness training to senior executives and military Defence Attaches in the Region; a role which he continues to deliver today. Edward lives in Bahrain and still enjoys cooking.

www.ingramcontent.com/pod-product-compliance
Lightning Source LLC
Chambersburg PA
CBHW030304100526
44590CB00012B/519